LUNCH TO GO

LUNCH TO GO

Everyday packed lunches made easy

RYLAND PETERS & SMALL
LONDON • NEW YORK

Designers Geoff Borin and Paul Stradling
Editor Alice Sambrook
Head of Production Patricia Harrington
Creative Director Leslie Harrington
Editorial Director Julia Charles
Publisher Cindy Richards
Indexer Vanessa Bird
Cover illustration Sania_Sun/Adobe Stock

First published in 2016 as *Lunch on the Go*.
This revised edition published in 2023 by
Ryland Peters & Small
20–21 Jockey's Fields
London WC1R 4BW

and Ryland Peters & Small, Inc.
341 East 116th Street
New York NY 10029

www.rylandpeters.com

Recipe collection compiled by Alice Sambrook.
Text © Amanda Grant, Annie Rigg, Belinda Williams,
Carol Hilker, Claire Mcdonald, Dunja Gulin, Helen Graves,
Jenna Zoe, Jennie Shapter, Jenny Linford, Jordan Bourke,
Laura Washburn, Lucy Mcdonald, Louise Pickford,
Nicola Graimes, Tori Finch, Tori Haschka and Ryland
Peters & Small 2016, 2023.
Design and commissioned photographs © Ryland Peters
& Small 2016, 2023.

ISBN: 978-1-78879-500-5

10 9 8 7 6 5 4 3 2 1

Notes
* Both British (metric) and American (imperial plus US
cups) are included; however, its important not to alternate
between the two within a recipe.
* All eggs are medium (UK) or large (US), unless specified
as large, in which case US extra large should be used.
Uncooked or partially cooked eggs should not be served
to the very old, frail, young children, pregnant women or
those with compromised immune systems.
* Ovens should be preheated to the specified
temperatures. If using a fan-assisted oven, adjust
according to the manufacturer's instructions.
* For notes on food safety and reheating food see page 7.
* Always sterilize mason/kilner jars before use.

MIX
Paper from
responsible sources
FSC® C106563
www.fsc.org

Printed in China

CONTENTS

BEFORE YOU START

We all know the importance of eating a good breakfast, and enjoy looking forward to a nice dinner, but many of us neglect our lunch. Often it's a dull sandwich – packed or bought hastily and soon forgotten. But the lunch hour can be a restorative oasis in the middle of the day, refuelling and energizing us for the activity of the afternoon. Making your own lunch is the perfect way to ensure that it is tailor-made to suit your needs, whether counting calories, following a vegan, gluten-free or paleo diet, or simply after something both wholesome and delicious for yourself or your family.

We are surrounded by more lunch options than ever before, whether from a traditional sandwich bar, convenience store or shiny food truck, but more often than not a compromise of some sort is involved in the purchases we make: flavour combinations, portion size and nutritional content are all variables of personal preference that have been decided by somebody else. On the other hand, a homemade lunch, created with care just the way you like it, is a much more enticing prospect. As well as being more economical than buying lunch every day, it allows you to plan a wider variety of balanced meals that give you exactly what you need – and if you are being careful with your diet, it helps keep you on track, too. No risk of thinking you are making a righteous

choice, but actually eating something packed with hidden nasties. Whether a busy office worker, student, or eagerly hungry child, a packed lunch is a little slice of home: reassuring and comforting and just what you fancy. With more than 75 recipes to choose from, including salads, wraps, savouries, street food, sushi and bento boxes, there is plenty of inspiration in the pages that follow.

There are many suitable options for both meat eaters and vegetarians, but do think of the recipes as templates and feel free to adapt and develop them as you like: vary fillings, breads or toppings as needed to suit your dietary requirements.

Many of the recipes can be made with leftovers, and once you've grasped the basics of batch cooking and using your freezer to best advantage (see page 8) you'll be whipping up a tasty lunch in minutes.

With a little bit of thought and planning, packed lunches can be quick and easy to prepare – just invest in a lunchbox and a few key store cupboard provisions (see pages 8–9), and you'll be all set to pack tempting treats to eat for lunch every day. Getting children involved in choosing and packing their own lunchbox with a nice variety of foods is also a good way to engage their interest in lunch.

It doesn't have to stop at lunch, either; try making a tasty morsel from the Snacks chapter or baking a treat from the Something Sweet section as a welcome change from the usual pre-packaged confectionery.

If you are new to the idea of taking your own lunch, why not give it a try and see how much you enjoy it? Once you embrace lunch on the go, however you approach it there's no doubt that lunchtime will soon start looking a whole lot more delicious.

HINTS AND TIPS

Putting together a well-rounded lunch on the go needn't be time-consuming or tricky, or require much special equipment. All you need is something to transport it in – and even an old ice cream tub will do! Here are some hints and tips on how to make it as easy as possible.

Choose your receptacle wisely

Although nearly any receptacle will do, it is worth selecting a smallish, sturdy box with an airtight lid to keep your lunch fresh and avoid the risk of spillages. Good-quality clip-lock plastic boxes with small removeable inserts are available, and these are extremely versatile, perfect for packing dips and sprinkles separately. Tiffin tins and bento boxes are handy, too, for their separate compartments. Clean miniature jam jars or even travel-size toiletry bottles are useful for taking dressings and toppings, and large food jars or mason/kilner jars with lids can be good for salads (see pages 42, 45 and 46).

Pack your lunch with care

Choose a box that's only just big enough for your lunch without squashing it, as that will stop it from falling apart. If your box is too big for your sandwich, try wrapping the sandwich in greaseproof paper before packing it; this will help it keep its shape and prevent it drying out. Miniature cool bags with small ice packs are useful for keeping a lunch containing meat, fish or dairy products cool if you don't have access to a refrigerator; on hot days you could also try putting your bottle of water in the freezer, then packing it next to your lunch the next morning to help keep it cool. A small vacuum flask or insulated coffee cup can be great for keeping soups and stews hot if you don't have a microwave to hand at lunchtime.

Assemble it just before eating

Take anything that might make your lunch go soggy, such as a dressing or sauce, in a separate container and pour it over just before you eat. Leafy salads are always best dressed immediately before eating (but note that pasta, noodle or pulse salads are best dressed beforehand, to help them absorb the flavours and stop them sticking). For wraps such as the Avocado & Chickpea Wrap (see page 15) or delicate sandwiches, roll

or fold the bread or tortilla and wrap it in greaseproof paper, then pack it in a box with the fillings alongside, and roll or fill it just before eating. Salads can be assembled in layers, with the wetter items at the bottom, and then mixed together just before eating. Packed this way, most sandwiches and salads can be prepared the night before and simply grabbed from the refrigerator on your way out. Don't forget to take a napkin or a travel pack of wipes for your hands.

Notes on food safety

If you have a microwave to hand, you may want to reheat some of the dishes in this book such as pasta bakes, soups or savouries. For best results, be sure to promptly cool and then refrigerate perishable leftovers after initially cooking. Then, always reheat thoroughly until the food is piping hot, taking special care over things like meat, fish and rice. It is good practice to cover food during heating and stir halfway through the cooking time if possible – both these things help to ensure the food is heated all the way through. Leave piping hot food to stand for a couple of minutes and then consume straight away. Never reheat food more than once, and discard any reheated leftovers. For more information on food safety, visit the Food Standards Agency (FSA) website in the UK or United States Department of Agriculture (USDA) website in the US.

Get crafty with your leftovers

It's no trouble to take leftovers for lunch, but if you think strategically you could make a little extra in order to lay in supplies for several lunches. Leftovers from Pulled Pork with Apple Butter (see page 29) are perfect in a sandwich, and leftover roast meat would be lovely in Sunday Leftover Sandwiches (see page 12) or in the Seared Lamb Salad with Pea, Mint & Radish (see page 56). Today's leftover roast vegetables could be the star of tomorrow's Salad of Roasted Root Vegetables (see page 59).

Make ahead in batches

Nothing could be simpler than making a batch of tasty soup, like the Roast Apple & Pumpkin Soup (see page 75) and storing it in portions in the fridge or freezer, along with small bags of the maple nut crumble to sprinkle over. Try varying the toppings with nuts and seeds, yogurt, fresh herbs or even a spoonful of spicy chutney. A chicken can be roasted ahead, the meat shredded and stored in batches to be used in countless salads or sandwiches, such as the Chicken Caesar Wraps (see page 20) or the Mexican Olé Bento Box (see page 67). If you have access to a microwave, you could make, portion and freeze a large batch of Cheesy Polenta & Roasted Vegetable Pie (see page 87) and enjoy a comforting and nutritious lunch whenever you fancy it. A batch of Falafel (see page 32) or Root Vegetable Fritters (see page 113) will keep beautifully in the freezer, too.

Work your freezer

When it comes to making regular lunches on the go, your freezer is your best friend. As well as making ahead in batches and storing leftovers, it's also great for storing baked goods, wraps, rolls and bread – just pull out what you need the night before and it will be ready to pack in the morning. When freezing, make sure you portion things in advance (freezer bags are handy here), and label clearly with the date. To stop them sticking, spread out individual portions like rolls, falafels and fritters on a tray to freeze them, then bag them up once frozen.

THE LUNCH-ON-THE-GO CUPBOARD

The real secret of lunch on the go is to have a good range of store cupboard provisions to liven things up a little. A basic couscous and roasted vegetable salad will be perked up immeasurably by the addition of a little feta and harissa; a layer of mustard or black olive tapenade will enliven a roast chicken sandwich; a spoon of sundried tomato pesto and a jar of preserved artichokes turns leftover rice into a lovely salad. Here are some of the most useful things to keep on hand.

Extra-virgin olive oil

A drizzle of oil at the last minute improves nearly everything. Why not keep a small bottle at the office, along with some salt and pepper?

Flavoured oil

Oils infused with herbs, hazelnuts, lemon or chillies/chilies make for delicious dressings, or can be simply drizzled over salads or soups.

Mustard

The essentials are a good Dijon and wholegrain mustard, which are great in sandwiches with leftover roast meat, and in dressings for pasta and rice salads.

Mayonnaise

A squeezy bottle of mayo is an endlessly useful condiment to have to hand: add to tuna or eggs, or mix with chopped chicken and bacon for easy sandwich fillings. Handy flavoured versions like garlic or chilli/chili mayo are great for adding interest, too.

Spices

Some spices and spice blends are wonderful for sprinkling over salads and soups. Try sumac for a spritz of acidity; dukkah (a blend of cumin and coriander with crushed nuts and sesame seeds) for a delicious injection of Middle Eastern flavour; or Turkish chilli/hot red pepper flakes to lift just about anything. A selection of freeze-dried herbs are also handy.

Dried fruit, seeds and nuts

These are lovely to sprinkle over salads and soups for a shot of extra crunch and nutrition. Dried cranberries, golden sultanas, pumpkin seeds, toasted sesame or chia seeds and pine nuts are especially good – experiment to find your favourite mixture.

Pickled vegetables

Explore the pickles aisle of your local grocer or supermarket and you'll find plenty to discover, and a dose of pickled capers or cornichons, tiny pickled onions or pickled chillies/chiles will invigorate your lunch.

Chutneys and relishes

From red onion chutney or cranberry relish to piccalilli, chutneys and relishes are more versatile than you might think. Try adding your favourite to a bowl of root vegetable soup, or to a wrap with rocket/arugula and leftover roast meat or ham.

Bottled sauces

Sauces can add invaluable piquancy to leftovers. There are as many varieties as there are preferences; some useful examples to try are chilli/chili sauce, tahini (great mixed with yogurt as a dip), herb pestos, harissa, tapenade and hoisin sauce.

Canned vegetables, fish and pulses

Preserved chargrilled artichokes or red (bell) peppers are a welcome addition to a summer salad; a drained can of cooked beans or pack of pre-cooked lentils adds protein; a good-quality can of salmon or tuna is a useful shortcut to a Niçoise-style salad. Olives of all colours and sizes are indispensable, too.

Brined cheese

Not strictly a store cupboard item since its shelf life isn't indefinite, brined cheeses such as feta and halloumi are nevertheless excellent to keep on hand – they keep for weeks before opening, and work brilliantly crumbled or diced over soups and in salads and wraps.

Garlic

One little clove goes a long way to really bring out the flavour in most dishes. Add it when cooking soups, roasting meat or making dips. Garlic salt or granules are perfect easy options for sprinkling on snacks like savoury popcorn (see page 122) or crispy kale (see page 120).

SANDWICHES, WRAPS & ROLLS

Leftovers from Sunday dinner can be transformed into delicious, quick and easy sandwich fillers for a lunch to look forward to on Monday. Here are some ideas to make the most of any leftover meat.

SUNDAY LEFTOVER SANDWICHES

Each makes 1 serving

French-style Beef Sandwich

2 slices wholemeal/whole-wheat bread
a little softened butter
1–2 tablespoons good-quality mayonnaise
100 g/3½ oz. leftover roast beef, thinly sliced
25 g/¾ oz. Roquefort cheese, at room temperature
2 cornichons, sliced
a handful of frisée lettuce

Spread the bread slices with butter and then spread with mayonnaise. Top with the beef slices, crumbled Roquefort cheese, cornichons and salad leaves. Sandwich together, wrap in greaseproof paper or clingfilm/plastic wrap and chill until required.

Southern-style Pork Bun

1 tablespoon sunflower oil
1 small onion, thinly sliced
2 tablespoons mayonnaise
¼ teaspoon smoked paprika
1 large brioche bun or roll
100 g/3½ oz. leftover roast pork, sliced thinly or shredded
25 g/¾ oz. shredded or finely grated carrot
a handful of salad leaves
salt

Heat the oil in a small frying pan/skillet and gently fry the onions with a little salt for 10–12 minutes until soft and golden. Drain on paper towels and cool.
Combine the mayonnaise and smoked paprika together.
Slice the brioche bun open and spread with the paprika mayonnaise. Fill with the pork, fried onions, shredded carrot and salad leaves. Wrap in greaseproof paper or clingfilm/plastic wrap and chill until required.

Asian Chicken Baguette

1 medium baguette
100 g/3½ oz. leftover roast chicken, shredded
a handful of mixed Thai herbs, (such as Thai basil, mint and coriander/cilantro)
a handful of mixed salad leaves
2 tablespoons sweet chilli/chili sauce

Slice the baguette in half and fill with the chicken, herbs, salad leaves and sweet chilli/chili sauce. Wrap in greaseproof paper or clingfilm/plastic wrap and chill until required.

Wraps make a pleasant change from ordinary sandwiches. If wholemeal/whole-wheat tortillas are available, they are the healthiest choice. This is a fairly sophisticated filling which may not appeal to all ages; for something simpler, try a basic combination of cream cheese and avocado slices.

AVOCADO & CHICKPEA WRAPS

4 wholemeal/whole-wheat tortillas or other wraps

400-g/14-oz. can chickpeas drained and rinsed

4 generous spoonfuls cottage cheese

1 ripe avocado, thinly sliced

1 tomato, deseeded and flesh diced

3–4 tablespoons grated Cheddar cheese

a few handfuls of shredded little gem lettuce and/or sprouted seeds

a little freshly squeezed lemon juice

salt and freshly ground black pepper

Makes 4 servings

Working one at a time, put a tortilla onto the work surface. Sprinkle a quarter of the chickpeas on top in a line down the middle. Mash with a fork, spreading in a half-moon shape towards one edge of the tortilla.

Cover this with a generous spoonful of cottage cheese. Arrange a few avocado slices on top, in a line down the middle.

Sprinkle over a small handful of diced tomato, a little grated Cheddar cheese and some lettuce and/or sprouted seeds.

Squeeze over a little lemon juice and season lightly.

Starting from the edge with the filling, begin rolling to enclose the filling. Wrap in greaseproof paper or clingfilm/plastic wrap and chill in the refrigerator until required.

Variations

Cream Cheese & Barley Spread
Make a spread using 200 g/1 cup cream cheese mixed with 200 g/1 cup cooked barley. Season with a pinch of celery salt and a pinch of garlic granules. Spread on a wrap and top with thin strips of celery, red (bell) pepper, shredded lettuce and grated carrot. Sprinkle with grated cheese, add a squeeze of fresh lemon juice and roll up.

Tofu Salad
Mash some firm tofu in a bowl with a few spoonfuls of mayonnaise. Stir in some finely chopped celery, thinly sliced spring onions/scallions, finely grated cheese and a pinch of dry mustard powder. Season lightly with salt and pepper. Spread on a wrap, top with sprouted seeds or shredded lettuce and roll up.

Egg, Cheese & Tomato
Spread some freshly prepared scrambled eggs or egg mayonnaise over a wrap, sprinkle with some finely grated cheese and diced tomatoes and roll up.

Perfect for lunch on the move, bagels are filling, sturdy and can be purchased in a variety of flavours including sesame, onion and jalapeño. Smoked salmon and cream cheese is a luxurious classic and an egg mayo bagel is great for brunch on the go too, if you tend to get hungry early.

SALMON & CREAM CHEESE BAGEL

(pictured)

1 plain white, poppy seed, onion or
    sesame seed bagel, cut in half
1–2 tablespoons cream cheese
3 slices smoked salmon
a few capers, rinsed and patted dry,
    or slivers of red onion (optional)
salt and freshly ground black pepper

Makes 1 serving

Toast the bagel halves and let them cool slightly before spreading one half with cream cheese.

Lay the smoked salmon slices on top and then add the capers or red onion. Top with the other half of the bagel and wrap in greaseproof paper or clingfilm/plastic wrap and chill until required.

EGG MAYONNAISE BAGEL

1 egg
1 plain wholemeal/whole-
    wheat, jalapeño, or
    sesame seed bagel,
    cut in half
2 teaspoons mayonnaise
a handful of fresh
    watercress
salt and freshly ground
    black pepper

Makes 1 serving

Place the egg in boiling water for 8 minutes until hard-boiled. Let cool for a minute, then peel and lightly mash it in a bowl using a fork. Add the mayonnaise and season to taste with salt and pepper. Mix together the ingredients, spoon into your chosen bagel and top with a handful of fresh watercress, then the other half of the bagel. Wrap in greaseproof paper or clingfilm/plastic wrap and chill in the refrigerator until required.

Variations

Egg with Red (bell) Pepper & Cucumber
Omit the watercress and add ¼ chopped red (bell) pepper and a little finely chopped cucumber to the egg mayonnaise mixture. Mix well, then spoon onto your chosen bagel and top with the other half.

Egg, Chives & Cress
Mix in a sprinkling of freshly snipped chives to the egg mayonnaise mixture. Instead of the watercress, add a handful of fresh cress, cutting from the bottom.

Egg, Bacon & Tomato
If you don't already have some cooked bacon to hand, you will need to turn on the grill/broiler to make this sandwich, so you may as well make at least enough bacon for two sandwiches to make it worthwhile. You do not need to add any mayonnaise, as the tomatoes add flavour and moisture. Grill/broil two bacon rashers/slices until crisp. Cut into small pieces. Hard boil two eggs and mash lightly in a bowl. Finely chop two tomatoes and add to the egg with the bacon. Mix, then spoon onto your chosen bagel.

This sandwich is tasty and satisfying but also healthy and suitable for vegans (if vegan bread is used). Ready-marinated tofu is widely available but you can of course also marinade your own and eat the fried cubes as snacks, too. Making sandwich spreads out of fresh vegetables is a great way to pack a diet full of nutrients whilst adding flavour and moisture.

FRIED TOFU SANDWICHES
with Roasted Romano Pepper Dip

240 g/8¼ oz. marinated tofu

sunflower oil, for frying

1 vegan baguette or 4 slices seeded bread
(optional)

sliced pickles or kimchi, to taste

2 handfuls of lettuce or other salad greens

4 tablespoons sprouted seeds

ROASTED ROMANO PEPPER DIP

1 kg/2¼ lbs. Romano peppers

150 g/¾ cup olive oil

4 garlic cloves, crushed

1 tablespoon apple cider vinegar

salt

Makes 2 servings

First make the roasted pepper dip. Preheat the oven to 180°C (350°F) Gas 4.

Place the peppers in a baking pan lined with baking parchment. Cook in the preheated oven, turning frequently, until the skin becomes black and blistery. Remove the peppers from the oven and place in an airtight container, covered, for long enough to build up the steam, about 15 minutes. Make sure you save the liquid that leaks from the peppers while cooling. Next, peel and deseed the peppers, again saving any liquid. Cut the flesh into small pieces. Heat the oil in a frying pan/skillet, add the peppers and garlic and fry for a couple of minutes with a pinch of salt. Add the vinegar, reserved pepper juice and more salt and sauté over a medium heat for another 20 minutes or until the juice has been absorbed and the mixture has thickened. Set aside to cool.

Cut the ready-marinated tofu into four 10-cm x 6-cm/4-in x 2½-in. slices, 6-mm/¼-inch. thick. Fry the cubes in a shallow layer of oil for 1–2 minutes, until golden brown, then drain on paper towels.

Cut the bread crossways in the middle, then lengthways to get two sandwiches. Add the cooled red pepper spread on the bottom slices, then add two slices of fried tofu, sprinkle with pickles, salad leaves and sprouted seeds and top with the remaining slices of bread.

Wrap in greaseproof paper or clingfilm/plastic wrap and chill until required.

Note: store leftover dip in an airtight container in the refrigerator and use within 2–3 days.

Store-bought chicken wraps are surely one of the most popular ready-made lunch options. The home-made version is so much tastier and fresher and there are loads of flavour combinations to try. Plus, you can keep an eye on everything that goes in, so there are no hidden high levels of salt or fat.

CHICKEN CAESAR WRAPS

75 g/2½ oz. Parmesan cheese

4 tortilla wraps

8–12 cos lettuce or romaine heart lettuce leaves, depending on size

300 g/10½ oz. cooked skinless chicken fillets, sliced

CAESAR DRESSING

2 garlic cloves, chopped

2 anchovy fillets in oil, drained and chopped

1 egg yolk

1 tablespoon white wine vinegar

1 tablespoon Dijon mustard

freshly ground black pepper

50 ml/⅓ cup light olive oil

50 ml/⅓ cup sunflower oil

Makes 4 servings

First make the Caesar dressing. Mash the garlic and anchovies to a paste in a small bowl. Put in a food processor with the egg yolk, vinegar, mustard and a little black pepper. Blend together briefly, then, with the motor still running, add the oils in a slow trickle through the feed tube, as if you were making mayonnaise.

Use a potato peeler to make Parmesan cheese shavings. Lay the tortilla wraps out on a clean work surface and top each one with 2–3 lettuce leaves, a few chicken breast slices and some Parmesan shavings. Drizzle with Caesar dressing.

Roll each wrap up tightly and cut in half diagonally. Wrap in foil or clingfilm/plastic wrap and chill in the refrigerator until required.

TURKEY & CRANBERRY WRAPS *(pictured)*

300 g/10½ oz. cooked turkey meat

3–4 tablespoons cranberry sauce

4 tortilla wraps

8 iceberg lettuce leaves, shredded

Makes 4 servings

Shred the cooked turkey meat using a fork. Spread some cranberry sauce onto a wrap and top with the turkey and shredded lettuce. Roll each wrap tightly and cut in half diagonally. Wrap in foil or clingfilm/plastic wrap and chill in the refrigerator until required.

Variations

Chicken with Mayonnaise, Yogurt, Raisins & Nuts
Finely dice two slices of cooked chicken breast and put into a bowl. Add a little mayonnaise, yogurt, a handful of raisins (or cranberries) and a handful of chopped nuts. Mix together and spoon into wraps.

Chicken with Mango Chutney & Cucumber
Shred a little cooked chicken and put into a wrap, top with a dollop of mango chutney and some thinly sliced cucumber.

Turkey with Spring Onions/scallions & Apple Sauce
Shred some cooked turkey meat. Spread a little apple sauce onto your wrap and scatter over the turkey. Top with ¼ chopped spring onion/scallion and roll each wrap tightly and cut in half diagonally. Wrap in foil or clingfilm/plastic wrap and chill in the refrigerator until required.

Nutrition Tip
Turkey is a good source of zinc – a mineral that helps aid digestion and maintain a healthy immune system. It is also important for healthy skin.

These fun wheels are colourful and exciting compared to a bland ham sandwich. Hopefully the fun novelty of eating wheels will be an interesting diversion for kids large and small. This recipe uses Swedish polar bread, if you can get hold of it, otherwise wheat tortilla wraps work just as well.

HAM, PICKLED GHERKIN & LETTUCE WHEELS

1 tablespoon cream cheese
2 teaspoons mayonnaise
6 sheets Swedish polar flatbread or wheat
   tortillas
6 iceberg lettuce leaves, whole
6 slices honey roast ham
3 gherkins/pickles, finely sliced lengthways

150 g/1⅓ cups grated mild Cheddar cheese
salt and freshly ground black pepper

cocktail sticks/toothpicks

Makes 6–8 servings

In a small bowl, mix the cream cheese and mayonnaise together.

Take a flatbread and spread over a small spoonful of the mayonnaise in a thin layer. Next, lay a lettuce leaf on top, followed by a slice of the ham. Place 2–3 gherkins/pickles along the middle and sprinkle over a large pinch of cheese. Lastly, season to taste with salt and pepper.

Starting from one side, roll up the flatbread and contents, using cocktail sticks/toothpicks to keep it in shape. Cut off either end to neaten, then cut the cylinder into 4–5 discs, like a sushi roll, removing the cocktail sticks/toothpicks as you go. Repeat with the remaining flatbreads. Wrap in foil or clingfilm/plastic wrap and chill in the refrigerator until required.

Grilled cheese for lunch is always such a treat, and here is one with a French twist. You can prepare this at home the night before like a normal sandwich and then pop in a toastie maker or cook inside a re-usable toastie bag in a toaster. For a really easy option you could always swap out the cooked leeks for ham or tomatoes.

LEEK & GRUYÈRE TOASTIE

1 large leek, rinsed and sliced thinly
   into rounds
1 teaspoon vegetable oil
1 tablespoon butter
½ teaspoon dried thyme
6 tablespoons dry white wine
4 slices white bread

a little softened butter
wholegrain Dijon mustard
250 g/2 cups grated Gruyère cheese
salt and freshly ground black pepper

Makes 2 servings

In a non-stick frying pan/skillet, combine the leek, oil, butter and thyme over a medium-high heat and cook, stirring occasionally, until soft and golden. Season well, add the wine and simmer until the liquid evaporates. Taste and adjust the seasoning. Set aside.

Butter each of the bread slices on one side, then spread two of the slices with mustard on the non-buttered side.

Spoon half of the leeks over each mustard covered slice and sprinkle over half the grated cheese in an even layer. Cover with another bread slice each.

Pop the sandwiches in plastic sandwich bags or wrap in clingfilm/plastic wrap and chill in the refrigerator until ready to use.

Cook in a toastie maker or in a re-usable toastie bag in the toaster. Transfer to a plate and cut in half. Let cool for a few minutes before serving.

Variation

Other good French cheeses to try here include Beaufort, Comté and Raclette.

Combining mozzarella with this intense, punchy Italian sauce is a match made in heaven. It is equally delicious eaten cold or warmed through and the flavours only intensify if left to chill overnight. A large focaccia sliced in half will make a delicious filling lunch for two or a lighter bite for four.

PUTTANESCA FOCACCIA

a large round or square focaccia, halved lengthways and widthways

extra virgin olive oil

4 tablespoons black olive paste

2 tablespoons sun-dried tomato paste

4–6 tablespoons passata/strained tomatoes

2 mozzarella balls, drained and thinly sliced

2 teaspoons dried oregano

2 tablespoons grated Parmesan cheese

2–3 tablespoons capers, drained

a good pinch of chilli/hot red pepper flakes

a few fresh basil leaves, torn

Makes 2–4 servings

Brush the outsides of the focaccia halves with olive oil and arrange oil-side down on a clean work surface or chopping board.

Spread two of the non-oiled sides generously with the olive paste. Spread the other two non-oiled sides with the sun-dried tomato paste, then top with the passata/strained tomatoes. Divide the mozzarella slices between the tomato-coated sides. Sprinkle over the oregano, Parmesan cheese, capers and chilli/hot red pepper flakes. Scatter over a few basil leaves. Top with the olive oil-coated bread, oiled side up.

Without turning the heat on, place the two sandwiches in a large, non-stick frying pan/skillet. If you can only fit one sandwich in your pan/skillet, you'll need to cook one sandwich at a time.

Turn the heat to medium and cook the first side for 4–5 minutes, then carefully turn with a large spatula and cook the other side for 2–3 minutes, pressing down gently with the spatula until golden brown all over.

Remove from the frying pan/skillet, transfer to a wooden chopping board or a large plate and cut the sandwiches in half. Leave to cool before wrapping in foil or clingfilm/plastic wrap and chill in the refrigerator until required. Eat cold or reheat until piping hot if desired (see page 7 for notes on food safety).

There is virtually no preparation to this recipe; the transformation from raw meat to food-of-the-gods is entirely due to sticking it in the oven. It's a fantastic meal to lazily eat with friends and family at the weekend and the leftovers are just ideal for a gourmet sandwich that will be the envy of everyone around, come weekday lunchtimes.

PULLED PORK ROLLS
with Apple Butter

3-kg/6½-lb. shoulder of pork, skin scored by your butcher
handful of sea salt
burger buns or bread rolls, to serve

APPLE BUTTER
a big knob/pat of butter
4 cooking apples, peeled, cored and chopped
2 teaspoons balsamic vinegar
2 teaspoons Dijon mustard
4 teaspoons dark muscovado sugar/dark brown molasses

Makes 10 servings

Preheat the oven to 125°C (250°F) Gas ½.

Place the pork in a large roasting pan, skin-side up. Rub the skin with paper towels to get it really dry. Take a scoop of salt and rub it over the skin, trying to get it into the scores carved by your butcher.

Cover the joint with foil and pop it in the oven for 9–24 hours (such flexibility!).

An hour or so before the end of cooking time, put the pork in a clean roasting pan without the foil (so the fat in the old pan doesn't burn and smoke out your kitchen).

Turn the oven temperature right up to 220°C (425°F) Gas 7 and let it cook for 30 minutes to brown the skin. If it hasn't puffed up enough to make good crackling, give it another 10 minutes, but keep an eye on it, as it can burn quite quickly at this stage. Take it out of the oven and let the joint rest until it is cool enough to 'pull' the meat off. Stuff the leftover pork into buns with apple butter.

Let cool before wrapping in greaseproof paper or clingfilm/plastic wrap and chill in the refrigerator until required.

Apple butter
Melt the butter in a saucepan and then add the cooking apples. Add the vinegar, mustard and sugar and let the apples cook away until they lose their shape and become similar to a purée. Give them a squash and a bash with a wooden spoon to help them on their way, and keep giving an occasional stir, for around 20 minutes, on a low heat.

Tip
If you do not have time to make the apple butter, just use normal butter for the roll and add a dollop of store-bought apple sauce to the rolls instead.

Bring some Mexican sunshine to lunchtimes with a quesadilla or a burrito. They are surprisingly delicious eaten warmed through or cold. Do try to put guacamole, sour cream or salsa in separate pots and add just before eating.

SWEET POTATO, SPINACH & GOAT'S CHEESE QUESADILLA

800 g/1 lb. 12 oz. sweet potatoes, cut into chunks

1 large chipotle chilli/chile in adobo sauce, finely chopped, plus 1 teaspoon of adobo sauce

200 g/3½ cups fresh spinach

8 large flour tortillas

150-g/5½-oz. log of goat's cheese, thinly sliced

vegetable oil

salt and freshly ground black pepper

TO ASSEMBLE (OPTIONAL)

sour cream

guacamole

salsa

Makes 8 servings

Preheat the oven to 120°C (250°F) Gas ½.

Boil, steam or roast the sweet potatoes until tender and leave to cool. When cool, mash the flesh with the chilli/chile and salt. Taste and adjust the seasoning and set aside. Put the spinach in a large saucepan, cover and set over a low heat just to wilt. Allow to cool, then squeeze out any excess moisture from the spinach using your hands. Chop finely and set aside.

To assemble the quesadillas, spread 2–3 tablespoons of sweet potato purée on 4 of the tortillas. Dot the spinach evenly over the surface and add a quarter of the cheese slices. Top with another tortilla.

Heat the remaining oil in a non-stick frying pan/skillet set over a medium heat. When hot, add a quesadilla, lower the heat and cook for 2–3 minutes until golden on one side and the cheese begins to melt. Turn over and cook the other side for 2–3 minutes.

Let cool before wrapping in foil or clingfilm/plastic wrap and chill in the refrigerator until required. When ready to eat, reheat until piping hot if desired (see page 7 for notes on food safety) or eat cold and top each quesadilla with sour cream, guacamole and salsa.

STEAK RANCHERO BURRITO *(pictured)*

1½ tablespoons olive oil

3 red (bell) peppers, sliced

2 medium onions, chopped

1½ tablespoons minced jalapeño peppers

4 garlic cloves, crushed

1½ tablespoons dried thyme

1½ tablespoons dried oregano

4 fresh bay leaves

½ teaspoon chilli/hot red pepper flakes

500 ml/2 cups beef stock

200 g/1 cup fresh tomatoes, diced

skirt steak, about 900 g/2 lbs., cooked and cut into pieces

500 g/4 cups long-grain rice, cooked

TO ASSEMBLE (OPTIONAL)

4 large flour tortillas

90 g/1 cup Cheddar cheese, grated

sour cream

few sprigs coriander/cilantro, chopped

a squeeze of lime juice

Makes 4 servings

Heat the oil in a large frying pan/skillet over a medium heat. Add the vegetables, garlic, herbs and spices and sauté for 5 minutes until soft. Add the beef stock and the diced tomatoes. Cook for another 4–5 minutes and add the steak and rice to the sauce for another 1–2 minutes. Leave to cool.

To assemble, fill each tortilla wrap with the steak, rice and sauce mixture and fold to seal. Wrap in foil or clingfilm/plastic wrap and chill in the refrigerator until required. When ready to eat, reheat until piping hot if desired (see page 7 for notes on food safety) or eat cold and top with cheese, sour cream and a few sprigs of coriander/cilantro. Finish with a squeeze of fresh lime juice, if desired.

Tip
As always, use whatever is easiest and what you have to hand. You can use leftover roasted vegetables from dinner or ready-cooked meat for a really easy option. Garnishes and choice of Mexican dips are all optional.

New York's famous Reuben sandwich is a lunchtime classic made famous by one of the city's numerous delis. It has been given many makeovers over the years but the basic components of rye bread, peppery pastrami and piquant Russian dressing remain an unbeatable and easy combination.

THE NEW YORK DELI SANDWICH

4 slices good-quality rye bread
6 slices pastrami
2 tablespoons sauerkraut
1 gherkin/pickle, finely sliced
75 g/2½ oz. Gruyère cheese, sliced
salt and freshly ground black
    pepper

RUSSIAN DRESSING
2 teaspoons mayonnaise
2 teaspoons tomato ketchup
1 teaspoon creamed horseradish
a pinch of mustard powder

Makes 2 servings

Start by making the Russian dressing. Whisk all the ingredients together in a small bowl and set aside until needed.

To build the sandwiches, start by spreading a generous layer of Russian dressing onto two slices of the bread. Add three slices of pastrami onto each slice, along with a good dollop of sauerkraut and a few slices of gherkin/pickle. Drizzle over a little more Russian dressing and top with slices of Gruyère cheese. Season to taste with salt and pepper, then top each stack with another slice of bread. Wrap in greaseproof paper or clingfilm/plastic wrap and chill in the refrigerator until required.

Middle Eastern falafel are classically served in pitta/pita, they are easy to make and taste great. This is a very quick and simple recipe for falafel, and it is a good way to encourage children to eat chickpeas.

FALAFEL POCKETS (pictured)

2 tablespoons olive oil
1 small onion, chopped
1 garlic clove, crushed
2 x 400-g/14-oz. cans cooked
    chickpeas, drained and rinsed
1 teaspoon ground cumin
1 teaspoon ground coriander

a handful of freshly chopped
    coriander/cilantro or mint
2 tablespoons mango chutney,
    plus extra to serve (optional)
freshly ground black pepper
plain/all-purpose flour,
    lightly seasoned

TO ASSEMBLE
4 pitta/pita pockets
lettuce, shredded
1 tomato, sliced

Makes 4 servings

Heat 1 tablespoon of the oil in a frying pan/skillet, add the onion and garlic and fry gently for about 5 minutes. Tip the onion and garlic into a bowl, add the chickpeas, cumin and ground coriander, then roughly whizz together with a hand-held blender.

Add the fresh coriander/cilantro and mango chutney and season with black pepper.

Mould the mixture into 12 balls and flatten into patty shapes. Dip them in the seasoned flour to lightly coat. Heat the remaining oil in the frying pan/skillet and fry the falafel on medium heat for 3 minutes on each side until golden brown. Let cool, then put into pitta/pita breads with the lettuce, tomato and extra mango chutney, if liked. Chill in the refrigerator until required.

Why make individual sandwiches for family members when you can make one giant sandwich and slice it up to share out? The ingredients are layered up inside the loaf, meaning you get a lot more bang for your buck when it comes to fillings. As with everything, the filling can be tailored to whatever ingredients happen to be in the refrigerator at the time.

PICNIC LOAF

2 courgettes/zucchini, sliced lengthwise
1 aubergine/eggplant, sliced lengthwise
1 red (bell) pepper, deseeded and quartered
1 yellow (bell) pepper, deseeded and quartered
1 garlic clove, crushed
olive oil
1 white cob loaf
a few tablespoons black olive tapenade or basil pesto

a few fresh basil leaves
10 slices salami
2 balls mozzarella cheese, drained, patted dry, and sliced
8 semi-dried (sun-blush) tomatoes, chopped
salt and freshly ground black pepper

a ridged griddle pan/stove top grill pan

Makes 4-6 servings

Mix all the vegetables with the crushed garlic and a glug of olive oil. Let everything marinate for about 30 minutes if possible. After this time, season the vegetables with salt and pepper, then heat a ridged griddle pan/stove top grill pan and cook the vegetables until soft and nicely charred in places. Set aside and leave to cool.

Cut off the top third of the loaf to make a lid. Hollow out the rest (bottom) of the loaf by pulling out most of the crumb from the inside with your hands. Leave a 3 cm/1¼ inch crust around the outside; it's important that this is a decent thickness so that it prevents the moisture from the vegetables turning the crust soggy.

Spread the inside of the loaf with the tapenade or pesto. Then, it's just a case of layering everything up inside. When the loaf is full, put the lid back on and wrap the whole thing tightly in clingfilm/plastic wrap. Weigh the loaf down by putting something heavy on top of it. Leave the loaf to press for a few hours at room temperature or in the refrigerator overnight before slicing into individual portions and wrapping in foil or clingfilm/plastic wrap. Chill in the refrigerator until required.

It is so easy to get bored of basic sandwiches at lunchtime. Why not treat yourself to this genius Indian-inspired meal? Spicy tandoori chicken, salty paneer cheese and fruity mango chutney, all wrapped up in a delightfully chewy naan bread. Some raita (homemade or store-bought), brought along separately in a small pot, is delightful for dipping.

TANDOORI CHICKEN & PANEER CHEESE NAAN-WICH

2 boneless skinless chicken breasts
    (about 300 g/10 oz.)
4–5 tablespoons tandoori paste
salt

Makes 2 servings

RAITA DIP (OPTIONAL)
½ cucumber, finely chopped
a handful of freshly chopped mint
a large pinch of salt
250 g/1 cup plus 2 tablespoons
    natural/plain yogurt

TO ASSEMBLE
a little butter, softened
2 large naan breads
2 thin slices mild cheese, such as
    Gouda or Fontina
4–6 tablespoons mango chutney
100 g/scant cup grated paneer cheese

Preheat the oven to 180°C (350°F) Gas 4.

Coat the chicken liberally with the tandoori paste, season lightly with salt and bake in the preheated oven for 20–25 minutes until cooked through. Leave to cool then cut into thin slices.

While the chicken is cooking, prepare the raita dip, by squeezing any excess moisture from the cucumber with paper towels and then mixing together all of the ingredients thoroughly. Set aside.

Butter the naan breads on one side and set aside. This is easiest if assembled in a large heavy-based non-stick frying pan/skillet. You'll need to cook the sandwiches in two batches, as naan breads are fairly large. Put one slice of bread in the pan/skillet, butter-side down. You will need to fold the bread over to form a sandwich, so position the filling on one side. Put one slice of cheese on the naan, then arrange half the chicken slices on top. Spoon over the chutney and spread out evenly. Sprinkle with half of the paneer. Fold one half of the bread over the top of the other half to cover.

Cook the first side over a medium heat for 3–5 minutes until deep golden, pressing gently with a spatula. Carefully turn and cook on the second side, for 2–3 minutes more or until deep golden brown all over.

Remove from the pan/skillet and leave to cool. Repeat for the remaining sandwich if necessary. Wrap in foil or clingfilm/plastic wrap and chill in the refrigerator until required. Eat cold or reheat until piping hot (see page 7 for notes on food safety).

It is amazing how the stylish Danes can even manage to make sandwiches appear almost like a modern art installation. Elegant and light, yet flavourful, these beautiful slices of rye bread topped with an assortment of ingredients make a great lunch. With this style of sandwich, it is best to pack the prepared components and assemble just before eating.

DANISH OPEN-FACED RYE SANDWICHES

½ red onion, very thinly sliced
1 tablespoon red wine vinegar
3 new potatoes
3 tablespoons good-quality
    mayonnaise
4 slices rye bread
½ avocado, stoned/pitted

a small handful of cress
2 baby gherkins/pickles, thinly sliced
1 radish, thinly sliced
1 teaspoon freshly snipped chives
2 asparagus spears, shaved into
    ribbons using a peeler

100 g/3½ oz. sliced smoked salmon
a small handful of fresh dill fronds/
    threads
salt and freshly ground black pepper

Makes 4 servings

Place the sliced red onion in a bowl and combine with the red wine vinegar. Leave to pickle and colour for at least 30 minutes. Put the new potatoes in a saucepan of lightly salted water and bring to the boil. Simmer until just tender, about 10 minutes depending on size. A sharp knife should glide in without much resistance. Drain and leave to cool. Slice the potatoes and avocado into 1-cm/⅛-inch thick slices.

Pack all the prepared sandwich toppings in a plastic bento box, using the separate compartments for each type of topping. Alternatively, pack in separate smaller plastic boxes, or wrap in clingfilm/plastic wrap inside one large box to keep the components separate. Chill until required.

When ready to assemble, spread a thin layer of mayonnaise on the four slices of rye bread, leaving the rest aside. Top two of the rye bread slices with layers of potato and avocado and sprinkle over a little salt

and pepper. Spoon some of the remaining mayonnaise across the centre of each slice of bread, then position the cress on top of the line of mayonnaise. Arrange a few slices of gherkin/pickles on top and scatter over some of the red onion slices and radish slices. Finally, sprinkle over the chives.

For the other two slices of rye bread, position the salmon onto the bread and spoon the remaining mayonnaise on top. Curl the shaved asparagus with your fingers and place on top, and finally finish with some dill fronds/threads. Season with a sprinkle of salt and black pepper and serve immediately.

Tip
As there are small quantities of asparagus, avocado, new potatoes, radish, gherkins/pickles, red onion and herbs used in this recipe, you could use any remaining ingredients to make a wonderful salad.

SALAD JARS, BOWLS & BENTOS

The choice of veg in this recipe should really be a selection of what you fancy and what's available. If you can, use produce in a variety of colours: it not only looks appetizing but also provides a wide range of nutrients.

SUNDAY MARKET SALAD JAR

150 g/5¼ oz. raw baby beetroot/beets,
    trimmed and scrubbed
7–8 radishes, trimmed
7–8 small tomatoes
a small handful of baby spinach leaves
¼ cucumber, peeled
75 g/2⅔ oz. buffalo mozzarella
½ teaspoon mustard seeds
3 tablespoons fruity olive oil
1 tablespoon freshly squeezed
    orange juice

1 teaspoon white wine vinegar
a small handful of fresh basil
salt and freshly ground black pepper

*a 1-litre/34-fl oz. mason/kilner jar with
    a lid*

Makes 1 serving

Place the beetroot/beets into a saucepan of cold water and bring to the boil. Cook for 30–40 minutes or until the beetroot/beets are tender when pierced with a knife. Drain and immerse in cold water. Leave to cool. Peel the beetroot/beets and cut into wedges or slices.

Cut the radishes into quarters. Cut the tomatoes into halves or quarters. Roughly shred the spinach leaves. Cut the cucumber into thick half slices and thinly slice the mozzarella.

Toast the mustard seeds in a dry frying pan/skillet until they start popping. Grind the seeds to a powder using a pestle and mortar or spice grinder and whisk together with the olive oil, orange juice and vinegar. Season to taste with salt and pepper.

Arrange the vegetables, basil and mozzarella in layers in the mason/kilner jar and pour over the dressing, shaking and tilting the jar so the dressing falls through the layers. Top with a round of baking parchment and seal. Chill in the refrigerator until required.

A lovely fresh-tasting, vibrant pasta lunch full of the colours of spring. If you don't have a spiralizer, simply grate the courgette/zucchini instead. Making pesto from scratch is so worth it – leftovers can be used for dinner.

SPRING PASTA SALAD JAR

100 g/1½ cups fusilli pasta

4 tablespoons extra virgin olive oil

75 g/½ cup podded fresh or frozen peas

a small handful of mangetout/snowpeas, trimmed

½ courgette/zucchini, trimmed

a small handful of rocket/arugula

50 g/⅓ cup pistachio nuts

2 tablespoons freshly chopped mint leaves

½ small garlic clove, crushed

freshly squeezed juice of ½ lemon

salt and freshly ground black pepper

a 1-litre/34-fl oz. mason/kilner jar with a lid

Makes 1 serving

Cook the pasta according to the instructions on the packet until al dente. Drain well and immediately refresh under cold water. Drain again and dry well. Combine with a little of the olive oil.

Blanch the peas in lightly salted, boiling water for 1 minute. Drain and refresh under cold water and drain again. Shake dry.

Thinly shred the mangetout/snowpeas and use a spiralizer (or grater) to spiralize or shred the courgette/zucchini.

Place the rocket/arugula, pistachio nuts, mint leaves, garlic, salt and pepper and half the remaining olive oil in a food processor and blend until smooth. Combine the remaining oil with the lemon juice and season to taste.

Arrange the pasta, vegetables and half the pesto in layers in the mason/kilner jar. Pour in the lemon dressing, cover the top with a round of baking parchment and seal the jar. Chill in the refrigerator until required.

Tip
This recipe makes twice the quantity of pesto needed, so use half and store the remaining half in an airtight container in the refrigerator for up to 3 days.

The mildly nutty flavour of quinoa goes with everything, and it's a great protein-rich, wheat-free alternative to pasta and rice for bulking up salads. Either cook from scratch following these recipes or buy it pre-cooked.

HERB & CITRUS QUINOA SALAD

300 g/1¾ cups uncooked quinoa

a handful of fresh basil, very finely chopped

a handful of fresh flat-leaf parsley, very finely chopped

a small handful of fresh mint, very finely chopped

2 garlic cloves, crushed

1 tablespoon capers, drained

freshly squeezed juice of 1 lemon

2 tablespoons olive oil

150 g/5½ oz. feta cheese, crumbled

salt and freshly ground black pepper

Makes 6 servings

Rinse the quinoa in a sieve/strainer under cold running water, then transfer to a saucepan. Cover with boiling water until just covered and set the saucepan over a medium heat. Cook for about 15–20 minutes, until the grains are tender, then drain and leave to cool in a mixing bowl.

Using the leaves of the herbs only, put the herbs, garlic and capers into a food processor and chop on a pulse setting, but make sure you don't purée the mixture. Add the lemon juice and olive oil and season to taste with salt and pepper. Pulse once or twice more until everything is combined.

Crumble the feta cheese over the cooled quinoa, pour over the herby dressing and mix together. Transfer portions of the quinoa salad to lunchboxes, then seal and chill in the refrigerator until required.

QUINOA SALAD JAR WITH MINT, ORANGE & BEETS *(pictured)*

4 medium beetroot/beets (about 400 g/14 oz.), scrubbed clean

extra virgin olive oil

1 tablespoon balsamic vinegar

300 g/1¾ cups uncooked quinoa

1 teaspoon fennel seeds

1 teaspoon cumin seeds

2 oranges, one zested

1 lemon, zested

a large handful of freshly chopped mint leaves, plus extra for serving

a small handful of freshly chopped flat-leaf parsley leaves

salt and freshly ground black pepper

4–6 x 0.5-litre/17-fl oz. mason/kilner jars with lids

Makes 4–6 servings

Preheat the oven to 200°C (400°F) Gas 6.

Trim the beetroot/beet stalks, but leave about 2.5 cm/ 1 inch on the top. Cut the beetroot/beets into 2-cm/¾-inch thick wedges, toss in 2 teaspoons of olive oil and season with salt and pepper. Place on a roasting tray and roast for 30–40 minutes until blistered and a sharp knife slides in with ease. Remove and toss with the balsamic vinegar while still hot.

Rinse the quinoa in a sieve/strainer under cold running water, then transfer to a saucepan. Cover with boiling water until just covered and set the saucepan over a medium heat. Cook for about 15–20 minutes, until the grains are tender, then drain well and leave to cool in a mixing bowl.

Place the fennel and cumin seeds in a dry frying pan/ skillet over a medium heat for a few minutes until aromatic. Turn off the heat.

Grate the zest of one orange and set aside. Then, cut the top and bottom off both oranges, just down to the flesh, then place the oranges on their ends, cut-side down, and carefully, following the shape of the orange, cut the skin off in strips from top to bottom, removing all the pith. Then segment the oranges by cutting the flesh away from the membrane. Reserve the juice that has come out during preparation.

In a large bowl, combine the cooked quinoa with the chopped herbs, spices, orange zest and lemon zest and season to taste with salt and pepper. Add in most of the beetroot/beets and orange segments (and reserved juice) and a little extra virgin olive oil. Combine and divide the quinoa salad between jars. Top each with the remaining beetroot/ beets, orange segments and a few fresh mint leaves. Top with rounds of baking parchment, seal and chill in the refrigerator until required.

Here are two quick, basic recipes which are both family favourites. Make a big batch – kids will enjoy a small portion on its own, but you can mix with salad leaves and add protein such as chicken pieces for greedy adults. For the pasta salad, try to use a small shape as it allows vegetables to nestle inside.

SIMPLE PASTA SALAD

200 g/3 cups pasta shapes

140 g/1 cups edamame or baby butter/lima beans, briefly boiled

165 g/1 generous cup cooked sweetcorn/corn kernels

2 carrots, grated

4–6 tablespoons mayonnaise

freshly squeezed juice of ½ lemon

a handful of freshly chopped flat-leaf parsley (optional)

salt and freshly ground black pepper

Makes 6-8 servings

Cook the pasta according to the instructions on the packet until al dente. Drain and let cool.

When cool, transfer to a bowl and add the edamame beans, sweetcorn/corn, carrots and mayonnaise and mix well. Add the lemon juice and parsley (if using) and season to taste.

Divide the pasta salad between lunchboxes, then seal and chill in the refrigerator until required.

Variation

Add tuna chunks, bits of ham, chicken or grated Cheddar cheese to bulk out for larger appetites.

SIMPLE COUSCOUS SALAD

225 g/1 cup whole–wheat couscous

400-g/14-oz. can cooked chickpeas, drained and rinsed

75 g/½ cup raisins

½ tablespoon freshly chopped flat-leaf parsley

½ red (bell) pepper, diced

a handful of pine kernels

freshly squeezed juice of ½–1 lemon

4–7 tablespoons extra virgin olive oil

salt and freshly ground black pepper

Makes 6-8 servings

Cook the couscous according to the instructions on the packet.

When cool, transfer to a large bowl. Add the chickpeas, raisins, parsley, red (bell) pepper and pine kernels. Squeeze in the juice of ½ a lemon and add 4 tablespoons of the oil. Season lightly and toss to blend. Taste, adding more lemon juice and oil as desired. Divide between lunchboxes, then seal and chill in the refrigerator until required.

Variation

Ingredients which can be finely diced and added in addition to, or to replace any in the basic recipe, include: celery, seeded cherry tomatoes, shallots, fennel, cooked butternut squash, pumpkin or sweet potato, orange segments and halved seedless grapes.

There are some days when we all need an extra boost, and this bowl full of ultra-healthy goodies is just the answer. For the best results keep the dressing separate and pour over just before serving.

'PICK ME UP' POWER BOWL

75 g/½ cup spelt berries

50 g/⅓ cup cooked
    chickpeas

2 tablespoons pumpkin
    seeds

½ crisp apple

½ avocado

2 tablespoons freshly
    squeezed lemon juice

2-cm/¾-inch piece fresh
    root ginger, peeled

2 tablespoons avocado oil

1 tablespoon sunflower oil

1 teaspoon runny honey

a handful of baby kale
    leaves

a handful of sprouted seeds

2 tablespoons dried
    cranberries

salt and freshly ground
    black pepper

Makes 1 serving

Place the spelt berries in a saucepan of cold water, bring to the boil and simmer gently for about 40 minutes until the berries are al dente. Drain, refresh under cold water and shake dry.

Drain the chickpeas, wash in a sieve/strainer and shake dry. Toast the pumpkin seeds in a dry frying pan/skillet for 2 minutes until they start to brown.

Cut the apple into thin batons. Peel, stone/pit and thinly slice the avocado. Add a little lemon juice to the apples and avocado and toss gently. This will help them to keep their colour.

Finely grate the ginger and combine with the avocado oil, sunflower oil, remaining lemon juice and honey. Season to taste with salt and pepper.

Arrange the ingredients neatly in a round plastic bowl or container, placing the sliced avocado on top with the cranberries. Chill in the refrigerator until required. Just before serving, drizzle over the dressing.

Tip
If it's possible, slice the apple and avocado just before serving to keep them extra fresh.

If you haven't discovered ready-cooked noodles in your local store, then that epiphany is alone worth the price of this book. They are part-cooked, which means they can be pan-fried in 90 seconds. So you can have packed lunch prep done in less time than it takes to make a cup of tea.

SPEEDY GONZALES NOODLES

garlic-infused oil
a handful of cooked frozen
    prawns/shrimp
a handful of frozen peas
300 g/10 oz. pre-cooked
    noodles
1 egg, beaten
soy sauce

*Makes 2 small or
1 large serving*

Heat a splash of garlic-infused oil in a large frying pan/skillet until hot.

Add the cooked frozen prawns/shrimp and peas and cook for about 2 minutes, then add the noodles and cook for another 90 seconds, stirring all the time. Stir in the egg and a splash of soy sauce to taste. This is salty so go easy for young children. Divide between lunchboxes, then seal and chill in the refrigerator until required.

Variations

Try replacing the peas with sweetcorn/corn kernels, carrot ribbons or bean sprouts. You can also use meat left over from Sunday's roast, shredded and added to the pan/skillet with the peas. Just make sure that it is properly heated through.

The salade Niçoise is an old favourite, the store-bought version of which can be of unpredictable quality. Make it yourself and you will be assured of its exquisite deliciousness. It evokes memories of a warm breeze coming off the Mediterranean and sand in between the toes, even if stuck at work.

PROPER SALADE NIÇOISE
with Roasted Vine Tomatoes

10 new potatoes, boiled and halved

225 g/½ lb. green beans, trimmed

325 g/¾ lb. vine tomatoes

75 g/½ cup black olives, stoned/pitted

2 tablespoons extra virgin olive oil

5 eggs, at room temperature

freshly squeezed juice of 1 lemon

4 x 175 g/6 oz. tuna steaks, 2.5-cm/
   1-inch thick

4 little gem/Bibb lettuce hearts,
   quartered lengthways

12 olive-oil-packed anchovies

a large handful of fresh basil leaves
   (optional)

salt and freshly ground black pepper

a ridged griddle pan/stove-top grill pan

VINAIGRETTE

a pinch of sea salt

3 tablespoons white wine vinegar

4 tablespoons extra virgin olive oil

1 generous teaspoon Dijon mustard

1 garlic clove, crushed (optional)

Makes 4–6 servings

Preheat the oven to 200°C (400°F) Gas 6.

Put the new potatoes in a lidded saucepan (preferably with a steaming basket attachment) and bring to the boil. After 10 minutes, add a steamer above the saucepan with the trimmed green beans in. Steam the beans for 4 minutes, then transfer them to a large roasting pan. Add the tomatoes (still on the vine) and olives to the roasting pan and drizzle over the olive oil. Cook in the preheated oven for 12–15 minutes.

Remove the potatoes from the boil (they should have had around 15 minutes total cooking time) and blanch in cold water to cool before draining and halving.

Boil the eggs for 6 minutes, then put the pan under cold running water for a couple of minutes to cool down. When cool, peel the eggs and cut them in half.

Transfer the roasted tomatoes, beans, olives and any warm olive oil to a dish to cool and squeeze over the juice of half a lemon and toss well.

Heat a ridged griddle pan/stove-top grill pan on the hob for 5 minutes. Brush the tuna steaks with olive oil and season really well with salt and pepper before placing the steaks in the pan. Cook for 3–4 minutes on each side, until the tuna is cooked through.

To assemble, divide the lettuce leaves between lunchboxes and scatter over new potatoes and anchovies, then add the halved boiled eggs, green beans, roasted tomatoes and olives. You can either choose to keep the tuna steaks whole and place them on the salad, or break them into flaky chunks and toss through. Seal the lunchboxes and chill in the refrigerator until required. Transport the vinaigrette separately and drizzle it over the salad just before serving, otherwise the leaves can wilt a little. Sprinkle with fresh basil leaves, if using, also just before serving.

Simple French Vinaigrette

To make the dressing, add a big pinch of sea salt to the vinegar and mix to dissolve. Add the olive oil, Dijon mustard and garlic, if using, and mix before sprinkling over the salad.

Pea, mint and lamb is a classic combination that works fantastically well in this salad. If fresh peas are in season, do make the most of them. Alternatively, frozen garden peas make a fine substitute.

SEARED LAMB SALAD
with Pea, Mint & Radish

2 tablespoons olive oil

2 teaspoons ground cumin

1 teaspoon paprika

350 g/12 oz. lamb steaks, fat trimmed

200 g/7 oz. shelled fresh or frozen peas, defrosted

100 g/3½ oz. radishes, sliced into rounds

a large handful of freshly chopped mint

3 tablespoons freshly snipped chives

100 g/3¾ oz. rocket/arugula leaves

lemon wedges, to serve

salt and freshly ground black pepper

DRESSING

3 tablespoons extra virgin olive oil

freshly squeezed juice of 1 small lemon

salt and freshly ground black pepper

a ridged griddle pan/stove-top grill pan

Makes 4 servings

Mix the olive oil with the cumin and paprika in a shallow dish. Season with salt and pepper, add the lamb and turn to coat it in the marinade. Leave to marinate for at least 15 minutes.

Cook the peas in boiling water for 1 minute until just tender, then drain, refresh under cold running water and drain again. Put the peas in a mixing bowl and add the sliced radishes.

Heat a ridged griddle pan/stove-top grill pan until very hot. Turn the lamb in the marinade then chargrill it for 2 minutes on each side or until cooked to your liking. Remove from the pan and leave to cool.

Mix together all the dressing ingredients, season to taste, and spoon it over the peas and radishes, then toss gently until combined. Stir in half of the mint and chives. To assemble, arrange the rocket/arugula in lunchboxes and top with the salad.

Cut the cooled lamb into diagonal slices and place on top of the salad with any juices. Arrange the remaining herbs over the top and add a lemon wedge to the lunchbox. Seal each lunchbox and chill in the refrigerator until required.

This hearty salad uses all those wonderful root vegetables with earthy flavours. It includes cubes of chorizo, but you can leave this out, if preferred. With or without the sausage, every mouthful of this salad is packed full of fantastic autumn flavours.

SALAD OF ROASTED ROOT VEGETABLES

2 beetroot/beets, peeled and sliced

2 parsnips, peeled and cut into batons

1 red onion, skin on, cut into wedges

½ small celeriac/celery root, peeled and thickly sliced

2 tablespoons olive oil

2–3 teaspoons runny honey

1 tablespoon fresh thyme leaves

a large handful of rocket/arugula leaves

1–2 teaspoons balsamic vinegar

75 g/2½ oz. goat's cheese, crumbled

1 cooking chorizo sausage (about 55 g/2 oz.), cubed (optional)

a handful of freshly chopped flat-leaf parsley

salt and freshly ground black pepper

Makes 2–4 servings

Preheat the oven to 200°C (400°F) Gas 6.

Put the chopped vegetables in a large baking pan, drizzle with the olive oil and honey, season with salt and pepper and sprinkle over the thyme leaves. Toss to coat the vegetables evenly, then pop the pan into the preheated oven to roast for 30–35 minutes, until the vegetables are golden brown and caramelized. Remove from the oven, toss again in the hot oil in the pan, then leave to cool.

In a frying pan/skillet, dry fry the cubes of chorizo sausage (if using) until lightly browned around the edges. Leave to cool.

Transfer the cooled vegetables to a large mixing bowl, making sure you discard the outer layer or two of red onion skin as you go. Add the chorizo and a little of the chorizo oil left in the pan/skillet. Toss in the rocket/arugula leaves, crumbled goat's cheese and balsamic vinegar. Season with salt and pepper and garnish with a generous sprinkling of parsley. Divide between lunchboxes, then seal and chill in the refrigerator until required.

Cauliflower takes on a new lease of life when marinated in spices and roasted until just tender. Here, it is served on top of an Indian-inspired chickpea, tomato and potato salad with a tangy tamarind and yogurt dressing.

CHICKPEA & SPICED CAULIFLOWER SALAD
with Tamarind Dressing

3 tablespoons cold-pressed rapeseed
   oil or light olive oil
2 teaspoons ground turmeric
2 tablespoons tikka spice mix
½ teaspoon curry paste
freshly squeezed juice ½ lime
1 cauliflower, cut into florets, stalks
   trimmed
400 g/14 oz. new potatoes, halved
400-g/14-oz. can cooked chickpeas,
   drained and rinsed
1 small red onion, diced
4 tomatoes, deseeded and diced

2 large handfuls of freshly chopped
   coriander/cilantro leaves
salt and freshly ground black pepper

TAMARIND DRESSING
3 tablespoons tamarind paste
2.5-cm/1-inch piece fresh root ginger,
   peeled and diced
freshly squeezed juice of ½ lime
6 tablespoons natural/plain yogurt

Makes 4 servings

Preheat the oven to 200°C (400°F) Gas 6. Mix together the oil, turmeric, tikka spice mix, curry paste and lime juice in a shallow bowl, then season. Add the cauliflower and turn to coat in the paste. Transfer to a roasting pan and cook for 10–15 minutes in the preheated oven, turning once, until tender.

Meanwhile, cook the potatoes in a pan of boiling water for 12–15 minutes, until tender. Drain and leave until cool enough to handle, then peel off the skins and cut into cubes. Mix together all the ingredients for the dressing and season with salt and pepper.

To assemble, put the potatoes in a large bowl with the chickpeas, onion, tomatoes and half the coriander/cilantro. Spoon the dressing over and mix gently until combined. Divide between lunchboxes, then top each with the roasted cauliflower and the remaining coriander/cilantro. Seal and chill in the refrigerator until required.

Tamarind
In its natural state, tamarind fruit looks like a long brown pod, inside of which is a sticky, tangy, seedy pulp. It's more commonly sold as a paste or in a block – with or without seeds – and adds a sweet-sour note to dishes.

This warm salad is packed with robust flavours as well as wholesome ingredients. The kale is roasted in the oven and is best kept crisp by packaging separately and adding to the salad just before you eat.

MARINATED MUSHROOM, CRISPY KALE & RICE SALAD

100 g/½ cup brown basmati rice, rinsed

1 teaspoon ground turmeric

3 tablespoons dark soy sauce

2 tablespoons sweet chilli/chili sauce

300 g/11 oz. chestnut or cremini mushrooms, sliced

175 g/6 oz. curly kale, tough stalks removed and leaves torn into large bite-sized pieces

2 teaspoons sesame oil

2 tablespoons coconut oil

2 handfuls of unsalted roasted cashew nuts, roughly chopped

salt and freshly ground black pepper

Makes 4 servings

Cook the rice following the packet instructions, stirring the turmeric into the cooking water. Drain, if necessary, and leave to stand, covered, for 10 minutes.

Meanwhile, mix together the soy sauce and sweet chilli/chili sauce in a bowl. Add the mushrooms and toss until coated in the marinade, then set aside.

Preheat the oven to 150°C (300°F) Gas 2. Toss the kale in the sesame oil and spread out on 1–2 baking sheets. Roast in the preheated oven for 15 minutes, turning once, until crisp but not browned; keep an eye on it as it can very easily burn.

Heat the coconut oil in a large frying pan/skillet over a medium-high heat and fry the mushrooms for 5 minutes. Pour off and retain any liquid from the mushrooms as this will form the dressing for the salad. Return the pan to the heat and cook the mushrooms for another 5 minutes, until they start to crisp.

Transfer the rice to a large bowl and add the mushrooms and the cooking juices. Stir until combined and season, if necessary. Divide between lunchboxes, then seal and chill in the refrigerator until required. Sprinkle each salad with the crispy kale and cashew nuts just before eating.

Bento boxes, originally associated with Japanese dishes, are a great way of incorporating a variety of tastes and textures into a meal and are ideal for a packed lunch. If you don't have a bento box, why not store the different components in individual containers inside one large container. As this meal contains raw fish, keep it well chilled and use a cool bag if possible.

ALOHA SEAFOOD BENTO BOX

1 teaspoon sunflower oil

100 g/½ cup jasmine rice

125 ml/½ cup coconut milk

a pinch of salt

125 g/4¼ oz. each fresh raw salmon and fresh raw tuna

1 spring onion/scallion, finely chopped

1 tablespoon light soy sauce

1 teaspoon mirin

½ teaspoon peeled and grated fresh root ginger

½ small pineapple, peeled and cut into wedges or slices, to serve

100 g/3½ oz. store-bought arame seaweed salad, to serve

1 tablespoon white and black sesame seeds

Makes 2 servings

Prepare the rice by rubbing the bottom of a heavy-based saucepan with the oil and top with the rice, coconut milk and 350 ml/1⅓ cups water and salt. Heat gently, stirring until the liquid starts to boil. Reduce the heat to low, cover and cook very gently for 15 minutes or until the liquid is absorbed. Remove from the heat but leave undisturbed until cold.

Dice the salmon and tuna and place them in a bowl with the spring onion/scallion. Stir in the soy sauce, mirin and grated ginger. Divide the fish mixture and add to bento boxes with two compartments. Add the pineapple wedges to the other compartments.

Pop the prepared seaweed salad into another bento box or plastic container. Top with the rice mixture shaped into a dome, if desired. Sprinkle the rice and seaweed with the white and black sesame seeds. Seal and chill in the refrigerator until required.

Tip

Either serve this as a lunch for two, sharing with a friend or divide ingredients in half and serve over consecutive days.

Mexican food doesn't have to be greasy and cheese-laden. This lunchtime bento box contains delicious marinated chicken thighs, a fresh corn and black bean salsa and all the trimmings for building your own light and healthy yet scrumptious burrito. Olé indeed!

MEXICAN OLÉ BENTO BOX

4 boneless raw chicken thigh fillets, skinned
1 small garlic clove, crushed
freshly grated zest of 1 lime
1 tablespoon olive oil
1 teaspoon agave syrup or honey
400-g/14-oz. can of black beans, drained
200-g/7-oz. can of sweetcorn/corn kernels, drained
2 tomatoes, diced
2 spring onions/scallions, finely sliced
2 tablespoons freshly chopped coriander/cilantro

4 jalapeños (optional)
4 corn tortillas
sour cream, to serve
lime wedges, to serve
salt and freshly ground black pepper

a ridged griddle pan/stove-top grill pan

Makes 2 servings

Combine the chicken, garlic, lime zest, oil, agave syrup or honey and a little salt in a bowl. Stir to coat the chicken.

Heat a ridged griddle pan/stove-top grill pan until hot, then carefully top with a sheet of baking parchment no larger than the surface of the pan (this cooks the chicken without it sticking to the griddle). Cook the chicken for 6–8 minutes each side until charred and cooked through. Leave to cool.

In a bowl combine the beans, sweetcorn/corn, tomatoes, spring onions/scallions and coriander/cilantro. Season to taste.

Take two bento boxes and divide each component between the boxes to give each some chicken, bean salad, jalapeños (if using), 2 tortillas, half the sour cream and some lime wedges. Seal and chill in the refrigerator until required.

This mini lunchtime mezze for one is full of lots of different Moroccan-inspired flavours as well as plenty of fresh fruit and vegetables. There are countless types of ready-made falafel available these days, but if you have time, do make up some of your own.

MOROCCAN MEZZE BOX

250 g/9 oz. store-bought falafel
  (or use the recipe on page 32)
½ red onion
1 small green (bell) pepper, deseeded
1 cucumber, deseeded
2 tomatoes
3 pitta/pita breads
3 tablespoons extra virgin olive oil
2 tablespoons freshly squeezed lemon juice
1 large carrot, peeled

1 small garlic clove, crushed
a small handful of pomegranate seeds
60 g/⅓ cup natural/plain yogurt
1 teaspoon tahini paste
2 tablespoons store-bought dukkah
  (a mixture of herbs, nuts, and spices)

Makes 2 servings

Cook the falafel following the recipe or instructions on the packet. Allow to cool.

Finely dice the onion, (bell) pepper, cucumber and tomatoes. Toast one of the pitta/pita breads until really crisp and let cool. Crumble into small pieces. Combine the pitta/pita, diced vegetables, one tablespoon of the oil and one tablespoon of the lemon juice. Stir well.

Finely grate the carrot and place in a bowl. Add the garlic, pomegranate seeds, remaining oil, lemon juice, salt and pepper.

Combine the yogurt and tahini, then season to taste and stir.

Divide the components into lunchboxes, so that each box contains both salads and the extra pitta/pita breads. Place the tahini yogurt and the dukkah in separate small pots, if possible. Seal and chill in the refrigerator until required.

SOUPS & HOT FOOD

Pot noodles, a favourite of students for decades, now don't have to be pre-packaged and full of E-numbers and additives – you can easily put together your own pot noodle with lovely fresh ingredients instead.

INSTANT CHICKEN 'POT' NOODLE

100 g/3½ oz. cooked chicken breast
   fillets
a small handful of dried black fungus
   mushrooms
50 g/1¾ oz. dried egg noodles
1 teaspoon sesame oil
1 spring onion/scallion, thinly sliced
4–5 mangetout/snowpeas, shredded

1 red chilli/chile, sliced
a handful of fresh coriander/cilantro
   leaves
2 tablespoons light soy sauce
½ chicken stock/bouillon cube

Makes 1 serving

Finely shred the chicken. Pour enough boiling water over the dried mushrooms to cover and leave to soak for 15 minutes until softened. Drain and slice thinly, discarding any tough stalks.

Cook the noodles according to the instructions on the packet. Drain, refresh under cold water and drain again. Dry well and combine with the sesame oil.

Arrange the noodles in a portable bowl or plastic container and top with the shredded chicken, mushrooms, spring onions/scallions, mangetout/snowpeas, chilli/chile and coriander/cilantro leaves.

Pour the soy sauce into the bowl and crumble over the half chicken stock/bouillon cube. Cover and chill in the refrigerator until required.

To serve, boil 500 ml /2 cups water in a kettle, pour over the dry ingredients and stir well until evenly combined and heated through.

Wholesome and sweet, you will thank yourself for making this nurturing autumnal pumpkin soup. The maple nut crumble is optional – the soup is just as nice eaten with some crusty bread. If you choose to top with cream or maple syrup, keep these separately in little pots until needed.

ROAST APPLE & PUMPKIN SOUP
with Maple Nut Crumble

4 Pink Lady apples, peeled, cored and roughly chopped into eighths

1.4 kg/3 lbs. pumpkin, skinned and chopped into pieces the same size as the apple

2 onions, quartered

a small piece of fresh root ginger, peeled and sliced

6 garlic cloves, skin on

4 tablespoons olive oil

1.5 litres/6 cups warm chicken or vegetable stock

2 tablespoons double/heavy cream, to serve (optional)

maple syrup, to serve (optional)

crusty bread, to serve (optional)

salt and freshly ground black pepper

MAPLE NUT CRUMBLE

120 g/¾ cup mixed nuts and seeds such as pumpkin seeds, hazelnuts, almonds and macadamia nuts

1 teaspoon salt

80 g/scant ½ cup caster/superfine sugar

Makes 4 servings

Preheat the oven to 200°C (400°F) Gas 6.

Put the apples, pumpkin, onions, ginger and garlic in a roasting pan. Drizzle with olive oil and season with salt and pepper. Roast for 45 minutes, until golden.

Remove from the oven. Squeeze the garlic from its skins and transfer the flesh to a saucepan. Add the contents of the roasting pan along with any pan juices. Process with a stick blender until very smooth. Season with salt and pepper. Pour hot straight into a vacuum flask or leave to cool, then cover and chill in the refrigerator until required. Reheat until piping hot when desired (see page 7 for notes on food safety).

For the maple nut crumble, dry-toast the nuts and seeds in a frying pan/skillet. Put onto a baking sheet lined with baking parchment and sprinkle with salt.

Put the sugar in a pan over a medium heat. Swirl the pan, rather than stirring, to mix the sugar as it melts. Cook until all the sugar has melted and has turned a light gold colour. Carefully pour the hot molten sugar over the top of the nuts. Transfer the baking sheet to the freezer and chill for 30 minutes. Remove from the freezer and roughly chop into pebbles.

If using, top the soup with the maple nut crumble, cream and maple syrup just before eating with crusty bread.

This soup is traditional and hearty, made from good, simple fare – defiantly unsophisticated yet delicious! There are two parts to the method, first a base to suspend the other ingredients, then a simple throw-it-all-in and simmer. If you have any left-over meat, or just a hankering for something carnivorous, you can add to the recipe – see variation below.

SCOTTISH ROOT VEGETABLE SOUP
with Pearl Barley & Thyme

100 g/7 tablespoons butter

1 small onion, diced

2 potatoes, peeled and diced

2 carrots, peeled and diced

800 ml/3¼ cups vegetable stock

1 parsnip, peeled and diced

¼ celeriac/celery root, peeled and diced

¼ swede/rutabaga, peeled and diced

2 celery sticks, sliced

1 leek, finely sliced

90 g/½ cup pearl barley

a handful of freshly chopped flat-leaf parsley

a bunch of fresh thyme, leaves only

100 ml/7 tablespoons double/heavy cream, to serve (optional)

salt and freshly ground black pepper

Makes 6 servings

Melt the butter in a large saucepan and add the onion, potatoes and half the diced carrots. Cook for a few minutes to soften, then pour in the stock. Cover the pan and bring to a boil, then simmer for about 15–20 minutes, until the vegetables are tender.

Draw the pan off the heat and blitz with a stick blender until very smooth.

Add the remaining vegetables to the soup base along with the barley. Cover the pan and simmer for about 7–10 minutes, until the barley and vegetables are tender. The barley naturally thickens the liquid, so keep an eye on it and top up with a little water if the soup begins to get too thick, or it will not cook properly and may catch on the base of the pan.

Once the vegetables are tender, stir in the herbs and season well with salt and pepper.

Pour hot straight into a vacuum flask or leave to cool then cover and chill in the refrigerator until required. Reheat until piping hot when desired (see page 7 for notes on food safety).

Just before serving, stir in the cream to just give that added richness, if you like.

Variation

For a meaty version, stir 250 g/9 oz. cooked pulled lamb into the soup when you add the herbs. Cook for a couple more minutes so that the lamb has a chance to heat through.

The hint of sweetness in this butternut squash soup makes it appealing to children. The vegetable and chicken broth with its chilli/chile and kaffir lime is perhaps suited to a more mature palate. Both options are delicious.

BUTTERNUT SQUASH SOUP

1 medium–large butternut
    squash
2 onions, cut into thin wedges
3 carrots, peeled and cut into
    thirds, widthways
2 celery sticks, cut in half

3 garlic cloves, skin on
1 tablespoon olive oil
750 ml–1 litre/3–4 cups boiling
    vegetable stock

freshly ground black pepper
a little runny honey

Makes 4 servings

Preheat the oven to 190°C (375°F) Gas 5.

Cut the butternut squash in half, scoop out the seeds and peel – you will need to use a sharp knife to cut the tough skin away. Cut the flesh into big pieces.

Put all the vegetables into a heavy-based roasting dish, add the garlic and drizzle over the oil and toss together. Roast in the preheated oven for 30–40 minutes.

Squeeze the garlic out of the skins and put into a food processor with the roasted vegetables and stock – you may need to do this in two batches. Alternatively, blend with a hand-held blender. Purée until smooth.

Pour into a saucepan, season to taste with black pepper and a little honey. Heat gently. Pour hot straight into a vacuum flask or leave to cool then cover and chill in the refrigerator until required. Reheat until piping hot when desired (see page 7 for notes on food safety).

VEGETABLE BROTH
with Chicken & Kaffir Lime (pictured)

1 tablespoon very light vegetable oil
4 chicken breasts, sliced into thin
    strips
8 spring onions/scallions, finely sliced
3 garlic cloves, crushed
2 green chillies/chiles, finely diced
2 lemongrass stalks, bashed to release
    their flavour
800 ml/3¼ cups vegetable stock
6 fresh kaffir lime leaves

1 small leek, white only, finely sliced
8 celery sticks, finely sliced
2 fennel bulbs, finely sliced
1 courgette/zucchini, finely sliced
200 g/1½ cups fresh or frozen peas
200 g/1⅓ cups skinned baby broad/
    fava or edamame beans
grated zest and freshly squeezed juice
    of 1½ limes, or to taste

a handful of freshly chopped
    flat-leaf parsley
a small handful of freshly chopped
    coriander/cilantro
a small handful of fresh mint,
    roughly chopped
salt

Makes 6 servings

Pour the oil into a large saucepan, pop in the chicken breast while the oil is still cold and stir to coat well. There is very little oil, so a fine coating on the chicken before the heat takes hold will prevent it sticking to the pan, and breaking up. (We don't want that, as this soup needs to be almost a clear broth with every exquisite element holding its own.)

As the pan begins to heat up, add the spring onion/scallion whites, garlic, green chillies/chiles and lemongrass. Toss around the pan for a couple of minutes, until the chicken becomes white around the outside, then pour on the stock. Add the lime leaves, leek, celery and fennel. Cover the pan and cook over a gentle heat for about 7–10 minutes, until the fennel becomes tender but not too soft. This soup needs to retain a little crunch.

At this point, remove the lime leaves and lemongrass if you feel their job is done, or leave them in if you want to make these flavours more pronounced.

Add the courgette/zucchini, peas and beans and cook for a further 3–5 minutes, until tender. Add the lime zest and half of the lime juice, taste, then add the rest of the juice if you feel it needs it, and season with a little salt. Once the flavour is pretty much where you want it, stir in the fresh herbs.

Pour hot into a vacuum flask or leave to cool, then cover and chill in the refrigerator until required. Reheat until piping hot when desired (see page 7 for notes on food safety).

Here are two supremely quick and easy soups, both popular with young vegetarians. The peanut and sweet potato is a surprising but pleasing combination. You can add less curry powder or chilli to taste. If nut allergies are a problem, omit the peanut butter and add a can of chickpeas.

AFRICAN PEANUT & SWEET POTATO SOUP (pictured)

2–3 tablespoons rapeseed oil

1 onion, chopped

2-cm/¾-inch piece fresh root ginger, peeled and grated

2 garlic cloves, crushed

¼ teaspoon dried chilli/hot red pepper flakes (optional)

2 tablespoons curry powder

3 medium sweet potatoes, peeled and diced

227-g/8-oz. can chopped tomatoes

1½ litres/6 cups vegetable stock

160 g/⅔ cup smooth peanut butter

200 ml/¾ cup coconut milk

salt and freshly ground black pepper

Makes 4-6 servings

Heat 2 tablespoons oil in a large saucepan. Add the onion and cook over a low heat for 5–8 minutes, until soft. Stir in the ginger, garlic, chilli/hot red pepper flakes and curry powder and cook, stirring for 1–2 minutes.

Stir in the sweet potatoes and tomatoes then add the stock. Simmer over a low heat for about 20 minutes, until the sweet potatoes are tender. Adjust seasoning to taste. Stir in the peanut butter and coconut milk and simmer gently for 10 minutes more. Pour hot into a vacuum flask or leave to cool then cover and chill in the refrigerator until required. Reheat until piping hot when desired (see page 7 for notes on food safety).

CREAMY COURGETTE/ ZUCCHINI SOUP (pictured)

1 onion, finely chopped

1 courgette/zucchini, grated

1 tablespoon rapeseed oil

1 litre/4 cups vegetable stock

a large handful of freshly chopped flat-leaf parsley

250 ml/1 cup silken tofu or milk (or half and half)

salt and freshly ground black pepper

Makes 4-6 servings

Combine the courgette/zucchini, onion and oil in a large saucepan and cook for 3–5 minutes, until soft. Season lightly.

Add the stock and parsley and simmer for 15–20 minutes, until the vegetables are tender. Stir in the tofu and cook to warm through. Taste and adjust the seasoning. Pour hot straight into a vacuum flask or leave to cool then cover and chill in the refrigerator until required. Reheat until piping hot when desired (see page 7 for notes on food safety).

Tomato-based soups such as these are good for all the family. Minestrone of course includes tiny pasta shapes, but you can add some cooked quinoa to the chicken and red pepper stew for a more substantial meal, if liked. Or wrap up and bring a small portion of crusty buttered bread for dunking.

CHICKEN & RED PEPPER STEW

2 tablespoons olive oil

8 boneless chicken thighs

2 onions, finely chopped

1 garlic clove, crushed

2 red (bell) peppers, deseeded and cut into bite-sized pieces

300 ml/1¼ cups chicken or vegetable stock

400-g/14-oz. can cannellini beans, drained and rinsed

freshly ground black pepper

a pinch of light brown soft sugar (optional)

a heavy-based casserole dish

Makes 4 servings

Preheat the oven to 180°C (350°F) Gas 4. Heat half the oil in a heavy-based casserole dish, fry the chicken thighs until lightly browned all over and transfer to a plate.

Add the remaining oil to the casserole dish, then add the onions, garlic and red (bell) pepper and fry gently for 10–15 minutes until very soft, but not brown.

Add the stock to the mixture in the casserole dish and cook in the preheated oven for 1 hour.

Spoon half of the sauce from the casserole dish into a jug/pitcher and blend with a stick blender until smooth.

Put back into the pan and add the cannellini beans and chicken. Cook for another 15 minutes until the chicken is cooked through. Cut the chicken into bite-sized pieces.

Season with black pepper and a pinch of light brown soft sugar, if using.

Pour hot straight into a vacuum flask or leave to cool, then cover and chill in the refrigerator until required. Reheat until piping hot when desired (see page 7 for notes on food safety).

CLARA'S MINESTRONE (pictured)

2–3 tablespoons extra virgin olive oil

1 onion, finely chopped

1 carrot, finely chopped

1 celery stick, finely chopped

1 leek, finely chopped

1 small courgette/zucchini, finely diced

75 g/¾ cup finely chopped mushrooms

1–2 garlic cloves, crushed

a splash of wine (optional)

1 litre/4 cups vegetable stock

a large handful of freshly chopped greens, such as spinach or kale

a handful of freshly chopped basil

250 ml/1 cup passata/strained tomatoes or 227-g/8-oz can chopped tomatoes

60 g/½ cup trimmed and diced green beans

50 g/¼ cup tiny pasta stars

100 g/½ cup cooked quinoa (optional)

finely grated Parmesan cheese, to serve (optional)

salt and freshly ground black pepper

Makes 4-6 servings

Heat the oil in a large saucepan and add the onion, carrot, celery, leek, courgette/zucchini and mushrooms. Cook over a low heat for 8–10 minutes, stirring often. Season depending upon the salt content of your stock. (If in doubt, season gradually and taste frequently.) Stir in the garlic. Add the wine (if using) and cook for 1–2 minutes, until evaporated.

Stir in the stock and greens. Add the basil and passata/strained tomatoes. Bring to the boil, then lower the heat and simmer for at least 15 minutes, until all the vegetables are just tender. Taste and adjust the seasoning.

Bring the soup back to a simmer. Add the green beans and pasta. Simmer for about 10 minutes, until the pasta is tender.

Pour hot straight into a vacuum flask or leave to cool then cover and chill in the refrigerator until required. Reheat until piping hot when desired (see page 7 for notes on food safety). Serve with the grated cheese for sprinkling, if liked.

Sweet potatoes are just as versatile as regular jacket potatoes and the sweetness goes well with salty ingredients like cheese and bacon. Here is a main recipe plus a couple of yummy alternatives to try for a lovely hot lunch. A microwave is essential, so this one is more for the workplace or students.

QUICK & EASY JACKET SWEET POTATO

2 rashers/slices smoked
    bacon
a 250–300 g/9–10½ oz.
    sweet potato, scrubbed
50 g/1¾ oz. camembert
    cheese, sliced
1–2 tablespoons
    caramelized onion jam/
    jelly
a little gem lettuce,
    shredded
a few ripe cherry tomatoes,
    halved
salt and freshly ground
    black pepper

Makes 1 serving

Grill/broil or fry the bacon rashers/slices until soft and golden. Leave to cool, then chill in the refrigerator until required.

When ready to eat, pierce the potato several times with a fork and place in the microwave. Cook on high for 3 minutes, turn the potato over and cook for a further 3–4 minutes until the flesh is really softened.

Cut a large slit into the potato and dot with the camembert and let sit for a minute for the cheese to melt.

Meanwhile, pop the bacon into the microwave and heat on high for 20–30 seconds until hot. Pop the bacon and onion jam/jelly into the potato, season with salt and pepper and serve with the shredded lettuce and tomatoes.

Variations

Tuna, Onion, Basil, Caper & Mayonnaise
Drain a can of tuna, finely chop a little red onion and finely chop a small handful of basil. Mix together with the capers and 1–2 level tablespoons mayonnaise to make a creamy filling. Pop some butter into the cooked potato and spoon in the filing. Scatter with some grated cheese to serve.

Beef, Sour Cream, Chive & Sweet Chilli/chili
Use leftover beef and slice thinly. Pop some butter into the hot potato and spoon in some sour cream and chopped chives. Arrange the sliced beef over the top and serve drizzled with sweet chilli/chili sauce.

Sometimes you just need a big comforting cheesy bake. These ones are meat-free and full of nutritious vegetables – so healthy as well as satisfying. They are easy to make and perfect for reheating for lunch the next day.

CHEESY POLENTA & ROASTED VEGETABLE PIE (pictured)

2 small courgettes/zucchini
1 red (bell) pepper
1 yellow (bell) pepper
300 g/10 oz. broccoli, sliced into long thin 'trees'
1 red onion, sliced into thick rings

extra virgin olive oil
salt
200 g/1⅓ cups quick-cook polenta
1 tablespoon butter
80 g/⅔ cup grated Cheddar cheese
125-g/4½-oz. mozzarella ball, sliced

a 25-cm/10-inch square or round baking dish, greased

Makes 6 servings

Preheat the oven to 200°C (400°F) Gas 6.

Cut the courgettes/zucchini in half widthwise, then halve lengthwise and cut into long thin fingers. Deseed the (bell) peppers then cut into thick slices. Spread the vegetables in a single layer on a baking sheet and add the broccoli and onion. Drizzle over 2–3 tablespoons of oil and toss to coat.

Season lightly with salt and roast in the preheated oven for 10–20 minutes, until just tender and lightly browned. You may need to roast in batches, depending on the size of your vegetables, and the broccoli may cook quicker. Check after 15 minutes and remove it if necessary, then continue cooking the other vegetables. Remove from the oven and transfer to the prepared dish.

Put 800 ml/3¼ cups water in a large saucepan, season lightly and add the polenta in a stream. Cook, whisking constantly, until thick. Take care as polenta can bubble up a bit ferociously.

When thick, lower the heat and continue cooking, stirring constantly, for 5 minutes more. Remove from the heat, then stir in the butter and grated cheese. Pour over the vegetables in the dish and spread out evenly with a spatula. Arrange the mozzarella slices on top and bake in the preheated oven for about 25 minutes, until browned and bubbling. Leave to cool, then decant into lunchboxes, seal and chill in the refrigerator until required. Reheat until piping hot (see page 7 for notes on food safety).

GNOCCHI BAKE

700 g/1½ lbs. store-bought gnocchi
680 g/2¾ cups passata/Italian strained tomatoes
a handful of sweetcorn/corn kernels
a handful of Swiss chard
200 g/2 scant cups shredded mozzarella cheese
a handful of breadcrumbs

Makes 4 servings

Preheat the oven to 180°C (350°F) Gas 4.

Cook the gnocchi in a saucepan of boiling salted water following the instructions on the packet. Drain and put back in the saucepan (not over the heat) and stir in the passata/strained tomatoes, sweetcorn/corn kernels and chard. Season to taste. Pour into a large baking dish and sprinkle over the mozzarella and breadcrumbs.

Bake in the preheated oven for 30–40 minutes, or until brown on top. Leave to cool then decant into lunchboxes, seal and chill in the refrigerator until required. Reheat until piping hot (see page 7 for notes on food safety).

The Indian tiffin box is a type of lunchbox used widely throughout Asia, which is usually made from stacked stainless steel compartments. Due to their durability, they have become popular worldwide and are now available in a range of shapes and sizes – they are the perfect carrier for a spicy lunch.

INDIAN TIFFIN BOX

DHAL

1 tablespoon sunflower oil

1 small onion, thinly sliced

1 garlic clove, crushed

2 teaspoons medium curry paste

100 g/½ cup dried red lentils

400 ml/1⅔ cups vegetable stock

1 tablespoon tomato purée/paste

200 g/2½ cups cauliflower florets

salt and freshly ground black pepper

TO ASSEMBLE

4 chapattis, paratha or 1 naan bread

a handful of fresh coriander/cilantro leaves

store-bought raita (or see recipe page 36)

2 tablespoons lime pickle or mango chutney

a handful of Bombay mix

lemon wedges

Makes 2 servings

To make the dhal, heat the oil in a saucepan and fry the onion, garlic and curry paste over a medium heat for 5 minutes. Add the lentils, stir well and pour in the stock, tomato purée/paste and salt and pepper. Bring to the boil, cover and simmer gently for 15 minutes. Add the cauliflower, return to the boil, cover and simmer for a further 5 minutes. Pour warm straight into a stainless steel tiffin box (which should keep the dhal warm for a few hours), or leave to cool and chill in the refrigerator until required.

Prepare the remaining ingredients. Divide the components between two tiffin box compartments (separate from the dhal) so each box has space for chapattis, coriander/cilantro leaves, raita, one or both chutneys, the Bombay mix and some lemon wedges. Seal and chill in the refrigerator until required.

Note

Proper tiffin boxes will not be suitable for microwaves, so if you need to reheat the dhal then decant into a microwave-safe container first and reheat until piping hot (see page 7 for notes on food safety).

Comfort eating is on offer here, with this satisfying version of the much-loved classic, mac n' cheese. Reheat and serve with a green side salad for a hearty lunch that you can look forward to all morning.

TOMATO MACARONI CHEESE

½ tablespoon olive oil

1 shallot or ½ onion, finely chopped

1 bay leaf

200-g/6½-oz. can chopped tomatoes

225 g/8 oz. dried macaroni or penne pasta

25 g/1½ tablespoons butter

25 g/2½ tablespoons plain/all-purpose flour

400 ml/1⅔ cups whole milk

salt and freshly ground black pepper

freshly grated nutmeg

75 g/1 cup Cheddar cheese, grated

8 cherry tomatoes, halved

10 g/3 tablespoons fresh breadcrumbs

salad leaves, to serve

Makes 4 servings

Heat the oil in a frying pan/skillet set over a medium heat. Add the shallot and bay leaf and fry, stirring, for 2 minutes, until the shallot has softened. Add the tomatoes, season with salt and pepper and fry, stirring now and then, for 2–3 minutes. Remove and discard the bay leaf, then blend until smooth.

Cook the macaroni in salted, boiling water until tender, then drain.

Preheat the grill/broiler to medium.

Make the cheese sauce by melting the butter in a heavy-bottomed saucepan or pot set over a medium heat. Stir in the flour and cook, stirring continuously, for 1 minute. Gradually pour in the milk, stirring all the time. Season well with salt, pepper and nutmeg. Bring to the boil, stirring all the time, reduce the heat and simmer until the sauce thickens. Stir in 25 g/⅓ cup of the Cheddar cheese until melted, then mix in the tomato sauce.

Place the cooked macaroni in a shallow, heatproof dish. Pour over the tomato–cheese sauce, mix well, then stir in the cherry tomatoes. Top with the remaining Cheddar cheese and the breadcrumbs, sprinkling evenly. Grill/broil for around 10 minutes, until golden-brown and bubbling.

Leave to cool, then divide between lunchboxes, seal and chill in the refrigerator until required. Reheat until piping hot (see page 7 for notes on food safety).

SAVOURIES

Ideal for popping in a lunchbox for a fuss-free snack, these cheese pastry recipes are not only quick, but tasty. You can make the pastry with most cheeses – Cheddar, Red Leicester or Parmesan all work really well.

PESTO CHEESE TWISTS

a little plain/all-purpose
flour, for dusting
375 g/13 oz. ready-rolled
puff pastry
about 80 g/2¾ oz. grated
cheese, e.g. Cheddar, Red
Leicester or Parmesan
2–3 tablespoons pesto

2 baking sheets, greased

Makes 30

Preheat the oven to 200°C (400°F) Gas 6.

Sprinkle the work surface with a little flour and spread out the pastry. Sprinkle the cheese evenly over half the pastry, then fold it in half. Using a rolling pin, roll the pastry out to its original size.

Using a palette knife, spread the pesto over half of the pastry and fold in half. Roll out to its original size. Cut into long, thin straw shapes.

Hold the end of a straw in one hand. Use your other hand to twist the other end of the straw to create a twisted shape. Lay it on the prepared baking sheet. Repeat with the other straws, leaving a little space between each one on the baking sheets.

Bake in the preheated oven for 8–10 minutes. Remove from the oven, carefully lift the straws off the baking sheet and transfer to a wire rack. Leave to cool and store at room temperature in an airtight container.

CHEESE STRAWS (pictured)

80 g/¾ cup plain/all-
purpose flour, plus extra
for dusting
3 tablespoons butter,
chilled and cut into small
pieces
40 g/1¼ oz. mature Cheddar
cheese, grated
1 egg, beaten

a baking sheet, greased

Makes 12

Preheat the oven to 180°C (350°F) Gas 4.

Sift the flour into a large bowl. Rub the butter into the flour using your fingertips until the mixture looks like fine breadcrumbs. Add the grated cheese and mix together. Add the beaten egg and stir into the flour until the mixture starts to come together. Then use your hands to work it into a ball. Sprinkle some flour onto the work surface and a rolling pin and roll out half the dough into a thin rectangle. Cut widthways into straws. Carefully lift them onto the prepared baking sheet, leaving a little space between each one. Bake in the preheated oven for 10 minutes, until golden.

Leave the straws to cool for a couple of minutes on the baking sheet and then carefully transfer them to a wire rack. Leave to cool completely and store at room temperature in an airtight container.

Sometimes the oldies are the best, and this super-healthy alternative to a traditional Scotch egg means you can indulge in childhood memories without the guilt of a deep-fried dish. The coating on the outside is a combination of chickpeas and minced/ground chicken with spices. The eggs are then baked rather than fried. Serve with a fresh green salad.

REALLY HEALTHY
SCOTCH EGGS
with a twist

125 g/1 cup cooked chickpeas

200 g/7 oz. minced/ground chicken

2 spring onions/scallions, chopped

1 garlic clove, crushed

1 tablespoon freshly chopped
   coriander/cilantro

½ teaspoon ground cumin

1 tablespoon tahini paste

a squeeze of lemon juice

5 eggs

30 g/3 tablespoons plain/all-purpose flour

50 g/¾ cup dried breadcrumbs

salt and freshly ground black pepper

a green salad, chopped cherry tomatoes,
   carrots and cucumber, to serve

a baking sheet, lined with baking parchment

Makes 4 servings

Preheat the oven to 190°C (375°F) Gas 5.

Place the drained chickpeas in a food processor with the minced/ground chicken, spring onions/scallions, garlic, coriander/cilantro, cumin, tahini, lemon juice and salt and pepper. Blend to a really smooth purée.

Place four of the eggs in a pan of cold water, bring to the boil and cook for 6 minutes. Immediately refresh the eggs in cold water. Peel the eggs carefully.

Whisk the remaining egg in a bowl. Place the flour on a plate and the breadcrumbs in a second bowl.

Using damp hands, take a quarter of the chicken mixture and flatten into a 12 cm/4¾ inch patty. Lightly flour an egg and place in the middle of the patty. Mould the mixture around the egg to fully enclose it. Press gently to neatly seal. Roll the patty in flour, dust off the excess, then dip into the beaten egg and finally roll in the breadcrumbs to completely coat the egg. Transfer the finished eggs to the prepared baking sheet.

Bake the eggs in the preheated oven for 40–45 minutes until golden. Chill in the refrigerator until required. Serve with salad.

Homemade sausage rolls are always a big hit with kids. These ones contain an additional boost of chopped red (bell) pepper and apple, they complement the other flavours well and contain plenty of vitamins.

SAUSAGE & RED PEPPER ROLLS

plain/all-purpose flour, for dusting

375 g/13 oz. ready-rolled puff pastry

1 tablespoon olive oil

1 onion, finely chopped

1 red (bell) pepper, deseeded and finely chopped

1 apple, cored and finely chopped

450 g/16 oz. good-quality pork sausagemeat

1 handful freshly chopped flat-leaf parsley (optional)

freshly ground black pepper

1 egg, beaten

ALTERNATIVE FILLING

450 g/16 oz. minced/ground chicken

1 tablespoon honey

2 teaspoons wholegrain mustard

2 large baking sheets, greased

Makes 18-20

Preheat the oven to 200°C (400°F) Gas 6.

Dust your work surface with a little flour and roll out the pastry until it is approximately 30 x 28 cm/12 x 11 inches and then cut in half lengthways.

Heat the oil in a frying pan/skillet, add the onion and (bell) pepper and sauté for 5 minutes until soft. Add the chopped apple and cook for 1 minute. Leave to cool slightly.

Put the sausagemeat into a bowl, add the onion mixture and parsley (if using) and season with a little freshly ground black pepper and mix together.

Divide the sausagemeat mixture into two equal halves and shape each into a long sausage shape. Place each sausage shape along the long edge of each piece of pastry. Brush the opposite edge of the pastry with beaten egg and roll up from the sausagemeat edge. Seal the pastry edges and turn the rolls over so that the seam is underneath.

Cut each roll into 2.5-cm/1-inch lengths. Cut a small slit in the top of each roll, brush with beaten egg and pop onto the prepared baking sheets. Bake in the preheated oven for 20–25 minutes. Remove from the oven, transfer to a wire rack and leave to cool. Chill in the refrigerator until required.

These dishes both make perfect light suppers, and the leftovers will keep well in the refrigerator overnight ready to pack into lunchboxes in the morning. Most children will enjoy nibbling the chicken off the bone, but you might like to cut the chicken off the bone and pack it in a pot.

SPINACH & ONION TORTILLA

5 eggs, beaten
2 tablespoons olive oil
1 large onion, halved and thinly sliced
175 g/6 oz. fresh spinach leaves, washed and chopped
40 g/½ cup Cheddar cheese, grated
salt and freshly ground black pepper

Makes 4 servings

Preheat the grill/broiler to high.

Break the eggs into a large bowl, season and beat briefly with a fork.

Heat the oil in a large frying pan/skillet with a heatproof handle and fry the onion until soft. Add the spinach and sauté for a couple of minutes to wilt the leaves.

Pour the egg mixture into the pan, turn the heat right down to its lowest setting and cook the tortilla, uncovered, for approximately 8 minutes, until there is only a little runny egg left on the top.

Sprinkle the grated cheese over the top and brown under the preheated grill/broiler for 1–2 minutes, until the top is golden and bubbling.

Use a palette knife to slide the tortilla out onto a plate. Cut into wedges. Leave to cool and then chill in the refrigerator until required.

CHICKEN DRUMSTICKS

8 chicken pieces (e.g. drumsticks, thighs, legs), skin removed
1 onion, finely chopped
8 tablespoons tomato ketchup
2 tablespoons soft dark brown sugar
1 tablespoon wholegrain mustard
1 tablespoon Worcestershire sauce
1 garlic clove, crushed

a heavy-based ovenproof dish

Makes 4 servings

Preheat the oven to 200°C (400°F) Gas 6.

Score the skin on each piece of chicken a few times. Put the onion into a large bowl, add all the other ingredients and mix well to form a marinade.

Add the chicken and stir really well until covered – you may prefer to use your hands to really work the marinade into the chicken. Cover and chill in the refrigerator for 15–30 minutes.

Put the chicken into a heavy-based ovenproof dish and roast in the preheated oven for 40–45 minutes. You may need to turn the chicken occasionally.

Leave to cool and then chill in the refrigerator until required.

Children love to help make the pastry for these savoury morsels – it is easy enough to rub the butter into the flour and roll and cut out the dough. Alternatively, buy some puff pastry and use this instead. Vary the filling – try tuna and sweetcorn, chopped bacon and cheese, or broccoli and salmon. If you don't have double/heavy cream, use another egg and a little extra milk.

MINI QUICHES

PASTRY

225 g/1¾ cups plain/all-purpose flour,
    plus extra for dusting
115 g/1 stick butter, chilled and cut
    into small pieces
1 egg yolk

FILLING

1 small onion, finely chopped
    (or 3 spring onions/scallions,
    finely chopped)
1 small garlic clove, crushed (optional)

1 tablespoon olive oil
1 egg, beaten
5 tablespoons double/heavy cream
5 tablespoons whole milk
2 skinless salmon fillets,
    cut into small cubes
a couple of handfuls finely grated
    Parmesan cheese

an 18-hole muffin pan, greased

Makes 18

Preheat the oven to 200°C (400°F) gas 6.

Sift the flour into a large mixing bowl, add the butter and egg and rub it in using your fingertips until the mixture looks like fine breadcrumbs.

Add 1–2 tablespoons water, a little at a time, stirring until the mixture comes together as a ball. Cover and chill in the refrigerator for 30 minutes.

Sprinkle the work surface and your rolling pin with a little flour and roll the pastry out thinly. Stamp out circles to fit your muffin pan using a glass or round pastry cutter. Lay the circles in the muffin pan holes and prick the base of each once with a fork.

Bake in the preheated oven for 5 minutes until the pastry is a very pale golden colour. Remove from the oven; leave the oven on.

Add the oil to a frying pan/skillet and gently fry the onion and garlic until soft.

In a jug/pitcher, mix together the egg, cream and milk. Divide the onion mixture and salmon between the baked pastry cases. Drizzle over the egg mixture, sprinkle with the Parmesan cheese and bake for 5–6 minutes until risen, slightly golden and set.

Remove from the oven and leave to cool for a few minutes before taking them out of the pan. Leave to cool and then chill in the refrigerator until required.

A slice of savoury tart is definitely up there with the most delicious of lunches. There are few who would turn down a bit of this one, the robust flavour from the chorizo permeates the egg filling and makes it so tasty. Slice into adult or child-sized portions and divide between lunchboxes.

LEEK, SPROUTING BROCCOLI & CHORIZO TART

PASTRY

225 g/1¾ cups white spelt flour

a pinch of sea salt

50 g/3 tablespoons cold butter

60 g/¼ cup cold hard white vegetable shortening (it is crucial that you get the hardest one you can find)

1 egg, beaten together with 1 teaspoon water

FILLING

3 leeks, finely chopped

1 onion, sliced

3 garlic cloves, crushed

10 spears of sprouting broccoli, bases trimmed

100 g/3½ oz. good-quality chorizo, skinned and chopped

3 eggs

7 tablespoons single/light cream

extra virgin olive oil

salt and freshly ground black pepper

a 20-cm/8-inch tart pan

baking beans

Makes 8-10 servings

Sift the flour and salt into a bowl. Cut the butter and shortening into small chunks with a knife and rub into the flour using your fingertips until it resembles breadcrumbs. Add a tablespoon of the egg mixture and fork the mixture together. If it is still crumbly, add a little more liquid. Bring the dough together to a smooth ball. Wrap in clingfilm/plastic wrap and chill in the refrigerator for at least 30 minutes.

Preheat the oven to 180°C (350°F) Gas 4.

Roll the pastry out until 1 cm/⅜ inch thick, working as quickly as possible. Line the tart pan evenly with the pastry, pushing into the corners of the pan and making sure there are no cracks. Prick the base with a fork. Line the pastry shell with baking parchment and fill with baking beans. Blind-bake in the preheated oven for about 20 minutes. Leave the oven on. Remove the paper and beans and brush with the egg mixture. Return to the oven and bake for a further 5–10 minutes until the base is beginning to brown. Remove and cool on a wire rack.

To make the filling, heat 3 tablespoons of oil in a large frying pan/skillet over medium heat. Add the leeks, onion, garlic, salt and pepper and fry until completely soft and translucent. After 10 minutes, add the sprouting broccoli spears. Heat another pan over medium heat. Add the chorizo to the dry pan and cook until a little crispy and the fat has seeped out. Add to the leek and broccoli and combine. Season to taste.

Preheat the oven to 200°C (400°F) Gas 6.

Add the cooked mixture to the blind-baked tart shell, reserving a little of the mixture for the top of the tart. Beat the eggs together with the cream and pour into the tart shell. Scatter the reserved ingredients over the top so they are completely visible, as this makes the tart much more attractive when it is cooked.

Bake the tart in the preheated oven for 30–35 minutes or until the top has slightly browned and is firm. Remove the tart from the oven and drizzle with a little olive oil. Leave to cool, then chill in the refrigerator until required.

Who doesn't love a savoury muffin? Great for grabbing on the go, these combine the rich, crumbly textures of feta cheese with the sweet, ripened flavour of sun-blush tomatoes. Enjoy alone or alongside a flask of soup.

BLUSH TOMATO & FETA MUFFINS

75 g/5 tablespoons butter, melted

2 eggs

140 ml/⅔ cup whole milk

300 g/2⅓ cups self-raising/rising flour

1 teaspoon baking powder

1 teaspoon salt

2–3 pinches of dried oregano

14 sun-blush tomatoes, chopped

100 g/3½ oz. feta cheese, diced

2 x 6-hole muffin pans, lined with
   10 muffin cases

Makes 10

Preheat the oven to 200°C (400°F) Gas 6.

Whisk together the melted butter, eggs and milk in a large mixing bowl.

In a separate bowl, sift the flour and baking powder together, then stir in the salt and oregano. Pour in the melted butter mixture and quickly and lightly fold into the flour. Stir through the tomatoes and feta cheese. Divide the mixture evenly between the muffin cases.

Bake in the preheated oven for 20–25 minutes until risen and golden-brown. Leave to cool completely and store at room temperature in an airtight container.

This is a great alternative to boring old bread. Its loaf shape makes it easy to toast – and it's good enough to eat for lunch on its own in thick slices. Just spread with butter and tomato chilli jam/jelly or top with cream cheese and ham, or anything you like.

COURGETTE/ZUCCHINI LOAF

300 g/3½ cups grated courgette/zucchini
300 g/2⅓ cups self-raising/rising flour, sifted
1 teaspoon baking powder
1 teaspoon mustard powder
½ teaspoon sea salt
½ teaspoon cayenne pepper
170 g/2 cups grated sharp Cheddar cheese
100 g/7 tablespoons butter, melted

4 eggs, beaten
135 ml/½ cup plus 1 tablespoon whole milk

a 900-g/2-lb. loaf pan, greased and lined with baking parchment

Makes 8 slices

Preheat the oven to 180°C (350°F) Gas 4.

Squeeze the grated courgette/zucchini with your hands to get rid of as much moisture as possible and place in a large mixing bowl with the flour, baking powder, mustard powder, salt, cayenne pepper and grated Cheddar cheese. Toss everything together gently with your hands.

Combine the melted butter with the beaten eggs and milk in a jug/pitcher. Pour over the courgette/zucchini mixture and gently combine using a large spoon. Take care not to overwork the mixture – you should have a thick batter.

Spoon the mixture into the prepared loaf pan and bake in the preheated oven for around 50–60 minutes, until golden brown and a skewer inserted into the middle comes out clean.

Set aside to cool in the pan for 5 minutes then turn out onto a wire rack to cool completely. Store at room temperature.

The idea of pizza for lunch will make both little kids and big kids jump for joy. This one is sneakily healthy, yet still satisfies those pizza cravings.

BROCCOLI, FETA & OLIVE WHOLE-WHEAT PIZZA SLICE

250 g/1¾ cups plus 2 tablespoons
   whole-wheat flour
1 teaspoon instant dried yeast
¼ teaspoon salt
150–160 ml/⅔ cup warm water
a small handful broccoli florets
50 g/1¾ oz. ready roasted (bell) peppers
   (from a jar or deli)
2 tablespoons sun-dried tomato paste
a small handful of stoned/pitted
   black olives

50 g/1¾ oz. feta cheese, crumbled
1 tablespoon pumpkin seeds
2 tablespoons grated Parmesan cheese
a handful of rocket/arugula leaves

Makes 2 servings

Sift the flour into a bowl and stir in the yeast and salt. Make a well in the middle and work in the warm water to form a soft dough.

Transfer to a lightly floured surface and knead for 5 minutes until smooth. Place in a lightly oiled clean bowl, cover with clingfilm/plastic wrap and leave to rise in a warm place for 1 hour until doubled in size.

Tip the dough out onto a lightly floured surface and roll out to fit in an 18 x 30 cm/7 x 12 inch baking pan, cover and leave to rise for 30 minutes.

Preheat the oven to 200°C (400°F) Gas 6. Meanwhile, blanch the broccoli in boiling salted water for 1 minute. Drain well.

Drain the (bell) peppers of any oil and slice thinly.

Spread the risen pizza base with the sun-dried tomato paste and scatter over the broccoli, (bell) peppers, olives, feta and pumpkin seeds. Scatter generously with the Parmesan cheese.

Transfer to the preheated oven and cook for 20 minutes until the base is cooked through and the topping browned. Leave to cool and then chill in the refrigerator until required. Cut in half and serve topped with rocket/arugula leaves.

These spiced golden fritters are a great way of using up leftover vegetables. They make a pleasant change from bready sandwiches – together with fresh salad leaves and a little pot of herby yogurt, they make for a dreamy lunch.

ROOT VEGETABLE FRITTERS
with Cumin & Parsley Yogurt

1 teaspoon cumin seeds

1 teaspoon coriander seeds

1 teaspoon mustard seeds

1 medium swede/rutabaga

2 large parsnips

extra virgin olive oil

2 tablespoons pure maple syrup

½ red onion

1–2 fresh red chillies/chiles, deseeded

½ teaspoon ground turmeric

a handful of fresh flat-leaf parsley leaves

3 eggs

2 small garlic cloves

1 teaspoon baking powder

2 teaspoons Dijon mustard

grated zest of 1 lemon

300 ml/1¼ cups plain yogurt mixed with
    1 teaspoon agave syrup, 1 teaspoon
    ground cumin and a small bunch of freshly
    chopped flat-leaf parsley

salt and freshly ground black pepper

green salad, to serve (optional)

Makes 4-6 servings

Preheat the oven to 200°C (400°F) Gas 6.

Put the cumin, coriander and mustard seeds in a dry frying pan/skillet and toast for 1–2 minutes until you can smell the aromas wafting up from the pan. Pound to a powder using a pestle and mortar.

Top, tail and peel the swede/rutabaga and parsnips. Cut into small chunks and toss in a bowl with a good glug of oil, a pinch of salt, maple syrup and the toasted spices.

Place in a roasting pan and roast in the preheated oven for 30 minutes, or until soft and slightly caramelized. Remove from the oven and allow to cool slightly.

Spoon all the roasted ingredients, the onion, chillies/chiles, turmeric, parsley, eggs, garlic, baking powder, mustard and lemon zest into a food processor and blitz until quite smooth. Season with salt and pepper.

In a large frying pan/skillet, heat 1 tablespoon of oil over medium heat. Drop heaped tablespoons of the blitzed mixture into the pan and flatten into round shapes. Fry for a few minutes on each side or until golden. Handle gently when flipping over, as they don't firm up until fully cooked. Let cool and chill in the refrigerator until required. Eat cold or reheat until piping hot (see page 7 for notes on food safety). Serve with the sweet cumin and parsley yogurt and a green salad.

Bulgur wheat is a healthy and fun alternative to rice in sushi rolls, but you could use either brown or white rice with this recipe if preferred. Either way, this veggie sushi is such a treat and not as hard as it looks.

ALTER-EGO SUSHI

200 g/1¼ cups bulgur wheat
a pinch of salt
1 tablespoon seasoned rice vinegar
1 small carrot, peeled
½ small cucumber, peeled
1 small avocado
4 sheets nori seaweed

4 tablespoons store-bought almond
    and parsley pesto
Japanese dipping sauce, to serve

a sushi mat

Makes 4 servings

Place the bulgur wheat in a saucepan with 500 ml/2 cups water and a pinch of salt. Heat gently until boiling. Cover with a tight fitting lid and cook over a very low heat for 20 minutes. Remove from the heat, drain any excess water and leave to go cold.

Transfer the cold bulgur wheat to a bowl and stir in the seasoned vinegar.

Cut the carrot and cucumber into equal sized 5 cm/2 inch batons. Peel, stone/pit and thinly slice the avocado.

Place a sushi mat on a flat surface with the slats going from left to right and top with a nori seaweed sheet. Take a quarter of the bulgur wheat and very carefully spread over the nori, leaving a 2-cm/¾-inch border at the side furthest from you. Build the bulgur wheat up slightly to form a mound in front of the clear border. Lay a quarter of the carrots, cucumber and avocado along the side nearest to you. Carefully spread the pesto along the top of the vegetables.

Very carefully pull the mat up and forward, rolling the seaweed and filling up tightly into a log, pressing firmly as you go all the way to the far side. Roll the mat completely around the sushi briefly to help seal. Remove the mat, wrap in clingfilm/plastic wrap and chill in the refrigerator until required.

Repeat with the remaining sushi to make 4 rolls in total. To serve, un-wrap from the clingfilm/plastic wrap and, using a sharp knife, cut into 6 thick pieces. Pack into lunchboxes along with pots of dipping sauce.

SNACKS

Chips and dips are *the* snack you just can't stop eating once you start. And with these wholesome versions of that moreish classic, there's no reason why you should stop – you can rest assured that you're eating only good stuff. Munch and crunch to your heart's content.

BAKED TORTILLA CHIPS
with Nectarine-tomato Salsa

10–12 all-corn tortillas
1 teaspoon sea salt

NECTARINE-TOMATO SALSA
1 nectarine
450 g/1 lb. cherry tomatoes
½ red onion
½ fresh jalapeño pepper (optional)
3 tablespoons freshly chopped
  coriander/cilantro
1 teaspoon chilli/chili powder
freshly squeezed juice of 1 lime
2 tablespoons apple cider vinegar

2 baking sheets, lined with foil

Makes 6-8 servings

Preheat the oven to 180°C (350°F) Gas 4.

Stack the tortillas on a board and cut through them into eighths to make wedges. Scatter the wedges over the prepared baking sheets and sprinkle with the salt. Bake in the preheated oven, one baking sheet at a time, for 13 minutes – don't bake both at the same time because the bottom sheet of tortillas will inevitably undercook. Thirteen minutes is the golden number – any longer and the tortillas will become impossible to chew; any less and they won't go crunchy. Store in an airtight container until required.

To make the salsa, dice the nectarine, cherry tomatoes, red onion and jalapeño, if using, and combine with the remaining ingredients. Now put half of the mixture in a food processor, blitz until smooth, then add it to the unblended mixture. This half-blending trick makes the perfect salsa – mostly smooth and easy to scoop onto a tortilla chip, but with enough chunks for you to be able to taste all the components. Chill in the refrigerator in an airtight container until required.

SEEDED AMARANTH CRACKERS
with Beetroot/beet & Herb Dip (pictured)

1 tablespoon melted coconut oil, plus
  extra for greasing
45 g/⅓ cup amaranth flour
40 g/⅓ cup milled linseeds/flaxseeds
40 g/¼ cup sunflower seeds
1 teaspoon sea salt
¼ teaspoon onion powder or
  ½ small chopped onion

20 g/⅛ cup pumpkin seeds
2 tablespoons milled hemp seeds
60 ml/¼ cup water

BEETROOT/BEET & HERB DIP
2 garlic bulbs, unpeeled
4 beetroot/beets, trimmed
3 tablespoons linseed/flaxseed oil
1½ teaspoons ground sumac

1 teaspoon cumin seeds
freshly squeezed juice of 1 lemon
1 teaspoon sea salt
freshly ground black pepper,
  to taste

2 baking sheets, lined with foil

Makes 4 servings

For the crackers, preheat the oven to 150°C (300°F) Gas 2. Grease one of the prepared baking sheets with a thin layer of coconut oil.

Pulse all of the dry ingredients in a food processor – you can leave the seeds in a roughly chopped state, if you prefer more texture. Then add the coconut oil and water and blend again until all the ingredients come together into a dough. Roll the dough thinly onto the prepared baking sheet and bake for 45–50 minutes. Set aside to cool, then break into pieces. Store in an airtight container until required.

To make the dip, preheat the oven to 180°C (350°F) Gas 4. Wrap the garlic in foil and put on one of the prepared baking sheets. Wrap the beetroot/beets in a separate sheet of foil and put on the same baking sheet. Roast the beetroot/beets and garlic for 30 minutes, then remove the garlic and set aside. Roast the beets for a further 30 minutes or until tender, allow to cool.

Peel the garlic and the beetroot/beets (this is the messy part so feel free to wear gloves!) and blend them in a food processor with the linseed/flaxseed oil, sumac, cumin seeds, lemon juice, salt and pepper. Add more linseed/flaxseed oil as required to reach the desired consistency. Chill in the refrigerator in an airtight container until required.

Kale chips have burst on the scene in a big way as a healthier alternative to processed, crunchy snack foods like potato chips. However, most commercial versions are coated with cashews, which makes them a lot more calorific than they could be. This yummy baked tomato version is fat-free.

SPICY TOMATO KALE CHIPS

1 head of curly kale or 1 bag
    of pre-chopped curly kale
    (about 50 g/1¾ oz.)
1 large tomato, quartered
3 sun-dried tomatoes
½ teaspoon paprika
¼ teaspoon ground cumin
a pinch of sea salt
⅛–¼ teaspoon cayenne
    pepper
freshly ground black
    pepper

a baking sheet lined with foil

Makes 2–4 servings

Preheat the oven to 200°C (400°F) Gas 6.

Tear small pieces of kale off the stems and place them in a colander. Wash them, then dry them as thoroughly as possible – ideally they should be completely dry. Place the dry pieces in a large bowl.

Put the tomato quarters and sun-dried tomatoes in a food processor. Pulse until smooth, scraping down the sides of the bowl as you go. It won't seem like a lot of mixture, but the idea is just to flavour the kale rather than cover it in a thick sauce. Add the paprika, cumin and salt, then as much cayenne and black pepper as you like, depending on how spicy you want your chips to turn out. Process the mixture again, then pour it into the bowl of kale. Using your hands, toss the kale so that it is evenly coated in the spice mixture.

Spread the kale pieces onto the prepared baking sheet and bake in the preheated oven with the door slightly ajar for about 14–16 minutes. You will know the kale is ready when it is totally crispy and thin. If you can resist eating it all immediately, it will keep in an airtight container for 4–5 days at room temperature.

These tiny pieces of cauliflower are dehydrated until crunchy, like popcorn. The creole rub is a mix of southern American flavours and adds a real zing. It takes about six hours in the oven or dehydrator, so make it ahead of time.

CREOLE CAULIFLOWER

1 large head of cauliflower, cut into florets about 1 cm/½ inch thick
2 tablespoons black treacle/ molasses or maple syrup
4–5 tablespoons passata/ strained tomatoes
1 teaspoon cayenne pepper
2 teaspoons paprika
1 teaspoon ground cumin
½ teaspoon dried thyme

½ teaspoon garlic powder
1 teaspoon sea salt
freshly ground black pepper

a baking sheet lined with baking parchment

Makes 3-4 servings

Preheat the oven to 115°C (225°F) Gas ¼, with the fan on if possible.

Wash the cauliflower florets thoroughly, then place in a large bowl. Put all the remaining ingredients in a separate, wide bowl and mix. Pour the mixture over the cauliflower in the bowl and toss until well coated.

Scatter the cauliflower on a baking sheet and bake in the preheated oven for about 6 hours, until thoroughly dried and crisp. Store in an airtight container for 4–5 days at room temperature.

Popcorn used to be just the treat you had occasionally at the cinema. It has now cemented its place on the supermarket shelves as a popular low-calorie snack. Making your own is so satisfying and simple. Try the luxurious and savoury cheesy truffle variation or treat the kids to a sweet vanilla and cinnamon alternative.

MASALA POPCORN

1 tablespoon corn kernels

½ teaspoon sea salt

1 tablespoon chaat masala (to make your own, mix a pinch each of garam masala, ground cumin, ground fennel seeds, ground ginger, black pepper and paprika)

Makes 1 serving

Put the corn kernels in a non-stick saucepan over medium heat and place the lid on top. As soon as you hear the corn start to pop, turn the heat down to low. Remove when all corn has popped – about 45–60 seconds.

Toss the freshly popped corn with the salt and chaat masala. Let cool and store in airtight container at room temperature.

Variations

Basil & Oregano

Add 1 teaspoon olive oil to the corn kernels in the pan. Pop as above, then remove from the heat and toss in 1 tablespoon each of dried basil and dried oregano.

Cheesy Truffle

Add 1 teaspoon truffle-infused olive oil to the corn kernels in the pan. Pop as above, then remove from the heat and toss in 3 teaspoons nutritional yeast, which will give the popcorn a slightly cheesy flavour.

Sweet Treat

Add 1 teaspoon coconut oil mixed with 1 teaspoon vanilla extract to the corn kernels in the pan. Pop as above, then remove from the heat and toss in a generous pinch of ground cinnamon.

Mackerel has the highest omega-3 content of all oily fish. Children need omega-3 for healthy brain function. Oily fish, like other fish, also contains essential minerals and protein and is a good source of vitamin D. You can serve this as a lunchbox snack in a couple of different ways. It can be used as a dip and eaten with vegetable sticks or fingers of toast, used to fill pitta/pita breads or rolls, or spread onto tortilla wraps.

SMOKED MACKEREL PÂTÉ

3 smoked mackerel fillets

4 heaped tablespoons natural/plain yogurt

1 garlic clove, roughly chopped

1 tablespoon wholegrain mustard or
    1–2 tablespoons horseradish (optional)

freshly squeezed juice of ½ lemon

freshly ground black pepper

vegetable sticks or toast fingers,
    to serve

Makes 4 small tubs

Remove the skin from the mackerel fillets and flake the fish into a food processor (or into a bowl if using a hand-held blender).

Add the yogurt, garlic, mustard and lemon juice and purée until smooth. Season to taste with a little freshly ground black pepper, if liked.

Put the dip into small airtight containers and store in the refrigerator, ready to serve. Cut up the desired number of vegetables or fingers to serve as an accompaniment. Store in the refrigerator in an airtight container. It will keep, chilled, for 2–3 days.

SOMETHING SWEET

These nifty little jars are great either eaten as brunch on the go, or serve perfectly as a healthy afternoon pick-me-up. Use any mixture of fruits, seeds or flavours of yogurt to create your ideal combination.

FRUIT, HONEY & YOGURT CRUNCH JARS

1 tablespoon sesame seeds

2½ tablespoons sunflower seeds

2 tablespoons maple syrup

2-cm/¾-inch piece fresh root ginger, peeled and grated

2 tablespoons brown sugar

freshly squeezed juice of ½ lime

500 g/1 lb. 2 oz. mixed summer berries, washed and drained

150 g/¾ cup Greek yogurt

2 x 0.5-litre/18 fl-oz. mason/ kilner jars

a baking sheet, lined with baking parchment

Makes 2 servings

Preheat the oven to 200°C (400°F) Gas 6.

Arrange the sesame seeds and sunflower seeds on the prepared baking sheet. Pour the maple syrup over the seeds, stir well until evenly coated and bake in the preheated oven for 6–8 minutes until golden. Leave to cool and crisp up. Break into small pieces.

Put the ginger in a small saucepan with the brown sugar, lime juice and 3 tablespoons water. Heat until boiling and then simmer gently for 5 minutes to make a thin syrup. Strain through a sieve/strainer to remove any bits and leave to cool.

Arrange half the fruit in the bottom of the mason/kilner jars. Pour in half the cooled syrup and then top with the yogurt and remaining syrup. Add another layer of fruit, then more yogurt and syrup (reserving any leftover syrup for another day). Seal and chill in the refrigerator until required.

Variations

Tropical Dream

Swap the mixed summer berries for diced kiwi, mango, pineapple and melon. Add a few drops of vanilla essence and a little honey to some Greek yogurt. Layer in jars and top with some toasted grated/shredded coconut.

Double Crunch Compote

Replace a third of the fruit with a layer of your favourite granola to add a wonderful crunch. Combine this in layers with fresh fruit of your choice, yogurt and some berry compote.

Refreshing, nostalgic and low in calories, what's not to love about jelly? Look out for sparkling juice drinks to make the fizzy versions. Whisking the jelly just before it sets traps the bubbles which gives them their 'fizz'.

FRESH FRUIT JELLIES

ORANGE
1 packet of orange jelly/Jello
1 tin mandarins or fresh satsumas

RASPBERRY
1 packet of raspberry jelly/Jello
1 can raspberries or fresh or frozen
    raspberries

LEMON
1 packet of lemon jelly/Jello
1 can citrus fruits or fresh orange,
    peach or apricots

STRAWBERRY
1 packet strawberry jelly/Jello
fresh or frozen strawberries
    or raspberries

5–6 small pots

Each makes 5-6 servings

If you are using canned fruits, melt the jelly/Jello with the recommended amount of water. Add the juice from the can of fruit and enough water to make it up to the right volume according to the instructions on the packet. If using fresh fruit, follow the packet instructions for the jelly/Jello.

Mash half the canned or fresh fruit to a pulp and add to the jelly/Jello. Divide the remaining fruits between the jelly moulds. Pour the fruity jelly/Jello mixture over the fruit in each mould and leave to set in the refrigerator overnight.

FIZZY FRUIT JELLIES

8 gelatine leaves
750 ml/3 cups either sparkling grape,
    raspberry or cranberry juice, or
    pomegranate lemonade
3–4 tablespoons caster/superfine sugar,
    or to taste

1 pomegranate, seeds scooped out
100 g/⅔ cup seedless red grapes, halved
100 g/¾ cup blueberries

6–8 small pots

Makes 6-8 servings

Soak the gelatine leaves in a bowl of cold water for 5 minutes.

Meanwhile, put 250 ml/1 cup of the juice and all the sugar in a saucepan. Place over medium heat until the mixture is just below boiling point.

Drain the gelatine leaves, add to the hot juice and stir well until the gelatine is thoroughly dissolved.

Pour the remaining juice into a large bowl, add the hot juice and gelatine mixture and mix well with a whisk to combine. Chill in the refrigerator until starting to set.

Meanwhile, set aside about 5 tablespoons of the pomegranate seeds. Mix together the remaining pomegranate seeds, the grapes and blueberries.

Once the jelly/Jello has started to set, you need to make it bubbly. Quickly whisk the jelly/Jello with a balloon whisk to make air bubbles. Fold in the fruit and divide between the 6–8 small pots.

Top the jellies with the reserved pomegranate seeds. Cover with clingfilm/plastic wrap and chill in the refrigerator until completely set.

Both these treats could be intended as breakfast offerings, and being homemade, they are not as sweet as regular bars or muffins. Combine with a piece of fresh fruit or some yogurt to round out the meal, or enjoy on their own as a nutritious, quick bite or afternoon snack.

APPLE & RAISIN MUFFINS

60 g/scant ½ cup plain/
   all-purpose flour
160 g/1 cup plus 2 tablespoons
   whole-wheat flour
110 g/½ cup packed dark brown
   soft sugar
1 teaspoon bicarbonate of soda/
   baking soda
½ teaspoon baking powder
1 teaspoon ground cinnamon
½ teaspoon ground allspice
a pinch of fine sea salt
250 ml/1 cup natural/plain
   yogurt, milk or buttermilk
3 tablespoons organic
   rapeseed oil

1 egg
4 tablespoons honey
100 g/⅔ cup raisins
1 small tart apple, cored
   and grated
1 teaspoon vanilla extract

*a 9-or 12-hole muffin pan,
   lined with paper cases*

*Makes 9 large muffins or
12 medium muffins*

Preheat the oven to 200°C (400°F) Gas 6.

Put the plain/all-purpose flour, whole-wheat flour, sugar, bicarbonate of soda/baking soda, baking powder, cinnamon, allspice and salt in a large mixing bowl and stir to combine.

Mix the yogurt, oil, egg and honey in a separate mixing bowl and beat until well blended. Stir in half the raisins, apple and vanilla extract.

Pour the yogurt mixture into the flour mixture and mix to combine. Divide between the paper cases, filling them almost to the top. Sprinkle the remaining raisins on top of each muffin.

Bake in the preheated oven for 25–35 minutes, until puffed and just brown around the edges. Let cool before serving. These muffins will keep for 2–3 days if stored in an airtight container.

CEREAL BARS

100 ml/⅔ cup sunflower oil
30 g/2 tablespoons light brown soft
   sugar
150 ml/7 tablespoons golden syrup/
   light corn syrup
250 g/2⅔ cups rolled oats
100 g/3½ oz. mixed seeds
60 g/3 oz. dried fruits (e.g. raisins,
   cranberries or chopped apricots)

a 20-cm/8-inch-square pan, greased

Makes 16

Preheat the oven to 180°C (350°F) Gas 4.

Put the oil, sugar and syrup into a saucepan and heat very gently to dissolve the sugar.

Add the rest of the ingredients and mix well. Tip into the prepared pan and bake for 15–18 minutes until set and golden. Leave to cool for 10 minutes, and then score into 16 bars.

Leave to cool completely in the pan, turn out and cut along the marks into 16 bars.

Store in an airtight container.

This is a super-virtuous version of the popular chewy cookie. It contains linseeds/flaxseeds, brown rice or quinoa flour, oats, coconut oil and raisins with only pure maple syrup to sweeten. It's not often you can congratulate yourself for eating a cookie as healthy as this, so you may as well have a few.

OATMEAL-RAISIN COOKIES

1 tablespoon ground linseeds/flaxseeds

100 g/¾ cup brown rice flour or quinoa flour

1½ teaspoons baking powder

½ teaspoon ground cinnamon

½ teaspoon salt

120 g/1¼ cups rolled or whole/jumbo oats

60 ml/¼ cup coconut oil

60 ml/¼ cup pure maple syrup

½ teaspoon vanilla extract

100 g/¾ cup raisins

a baking sheet, lined with foil

Makes 15-16

Preheat the oven to 180°C (350°F) Gas 4.

Combine 1 tablespoon ground linseeds/flaxseeds with 3 tablespoons cold water. Mix well with a fork and refrigerate until needed.

In a mixing bowl, sift together the flour, baking powder, cinnamon and salt. Stir in the oats.

Gently melt the coconut oil in a small saucepan set over a gentle heat until completely liquid and let cool. Stir in the maple syrup and vanilla extract. Remove the chilled linseed/flaxseed mixture from the fridge and mix it into the coconut and maple syrup mixture. Pour this wet mixture into the bowl of dry ingredients and incorporate well. Add the raisins and stir them in.

Spoon 2 heaped tablespoons of mixture onto the prepared baking sheet at a time, and press down gently with the back of the spoon to flatten. Bake the cookies in the preheated oven for about 12 minutes.

Remove the cookies from the oven and allow them to cool for at least 10 minutes to allow them to firm up nicely. Store in an airtight container for up to 4 days.

Here are two sweet treats which kids just adore, unapologetically a bit sugary but made from scratch, so still better than store-bought varieties. If you are a fan of sweet and salt in your treats, you will love the fun peanut butter and jelly cookies with a dollop of strawberry jam/jelly in the centre.

LEMON SHORTBREAD FINGERS

175 g/1½ sticks butter, softened

75 g/⅓ cup plus 2 tablespoons golden caster sugar, plus extra to dust

zest of 1 lemon

200 g/1½ cups plain/all-purpose flour

50 g/½ cup cornflour/cornstarch

a 20-cm/8-inch square pan, greased and base-lined

Makes 10-12

Preheat the oven to 190°C (375°F) Gas 5.

Beat the butter and sugar together until soft, pale and fluffy.

Add the lemon zest, flour and cornflour/cornstarch and mix again until it comes together.

Cover the bowl and chill the mixture in the refrigerator for 10 minutes, if you have the time. If not, you can cook it straight away – it will not make a big difference either way.

Press the dough into the prepared pan and bake for 15 minutes.

Remove from the oven and dust with sugar, if liked. Score the dough into about 12 fingers (score in half and then score each half into about 6 fingers) and leave to cool completely in the pan.

Once cool, cut into fingers and remove from the pan. Store in an airtight container for 3–4 days.

PEANUT BUTTER & JELLY THUMBPRINT COOKIES *(pictured)*

125 g/1 cup plain/all-purpose flour

¼ teaspoon salt

¼ teaspoon bicarbonate of soda/ baking soda

1 teaspoon baking powder

45 g/¼ cup caster/granulated sugar

60 ml/¼ cup pure maple syrup

1 teaspoon vanilla extract

5 tablespoons peanut butter

1½ tablespoons coconut oil

a few large tablespoons of good-quality strawberry jam/jelly

a baking sheet, lined with baking parchment

Makes 12

Preheat the oven to 180°C (350°F) Gas 4.

Sift together the flour, salt, bicarbonate of soda/baking soda and baking powder into a bowl. Add the sugar and stir.

Separately, combine the maple syrup, vanilla extract, peanut butter and coconut oil. Stir until the peanut butter has liquefied.

Add the wet mixture to the bowl of dry ingredients and incorporate well, but be sure not to overmix.

Pinch off small pieces of dough and roll into balls between your hands. Flatten them slightly between your palms and arrange them on the prepared baking sheet. Using the back of a teaspoon, press a small well in the middle of each cookie. Bake the cookies in the preheated oven for 10 minutes. Remove the baking sheet from the oven and spoon a little jam/jelly into the well in each cookie but don't fill them up to the top, as the jam/jelly will rise when heated. Return the baking sheet to the oven and bake for a further 5 minutes.

Remove the cookies from the oven and allow them to cool completely before eating. Store in an airtight container for up to 3 days.

No-bake crispie cakes are so simple to make and therefore great for getting young children interested in cooking. The healthy orange, cardamom and hemp muffins flavoured with warming cinnamon are perfect with a cup of tea or coffee. Both are equally handy for popping into a lunchbox.

NO-BAKE CRISPIE CAKES

100 g/3½ oz. dark/bittersweet
  chocolate, chopped
60 ml/¼ cup coconut oil or
  60 g/¼ cup non-hydrogenated
  sunflower spread
¼ teaspoon salt
110 g/2 cups plain corn flakes,
  with no added sugar

*2 x 12-hole muffin pans, lined with
  paper cases*

Makes 24

Put the chocolate, coconut oil and salt in a heatproof bowl over a saucepan of barely simmering water. Leave until melted and completely smooth.

    Tip the corn flakes into the melted chocolate. Mix thoroughly with a wooden spoon but don't be afraid to crush some of the corn flakes. Scoop a generous tablespoon of the mixture into each muffin case, patting the mixture down as you go. Put the whole muffin pans in the freezer for 15 minutes. Remove from the freezer and chill in the refrigerator until required. Alternatively, store in the refrigerator for up to 2 weeks.

ORANGE, CARDAMOM & HEMP-SEED MUFFINS

125 g/1 cup quinoa flour
½ teaspoon bicarbonate of soda/
  baking soda
1 teaspoon baking powder
½ teaspoon salt
1 teaspoon ground cardamom
1 teaspoon ground cinnamon
2–3 big tablespoons shelled
  hemp seeds

1–1½ teaspoons orange extract
  or orange oil
1 tablespoon apple cider vinegar
85 ml/⅓ cup unsweetened apple
  purée/applesauce
60 ml/¼ cup rice or almond milk
3 tablespoons pure maple syrup,
  or more apple purée/applesauce
2 tablespoons granulated
  sweetener

*24-hole mini muffin pan, lined with
  paper cases*

*Makes 24 mini muffins,
or 9-10 regular muffins*

Preheat the oven to 180°C (350°F) Gas 4.

In a bowl, combine the quinoa flour, bicarbonate of soda/baking soda, baking powder and salt, then sift in the cardamom and cinnamon. Add a generous portion of the shelled hemp seeds. There's no need to measure these – more hemp seeds will up the protein and healthy fats in your muffins.

Separately, mix together the orange extract, vinegar, apple purée/applesauce, milk, maple syrup and sweetener.

Mix the wet ingredients into the bowl of dry ingredients, but be sure not to overmix everything. Spoon the mixture into the muffin cases, filling them just three-quarters full, and level the tops with your index finger. Bake in the preheated oven for 8–10 minutes for mini muffins, and 9–12 minutes for regular muffins. It's fine to slightly under-bake these if you want them to be particularly moist on the inside, because none of the ingredients involved are harmful if consumed raw.

Allow the muffins to cool before eating or storing in an airtight container for up to 5 days.

An ultimate cake-on-the-go, this banana bread is perfect for munching on the bus, in the car, at school or at work. Whack the lid on, throw in a bag and enjoy home-baked cake anywhere you like. You can also cook this mixture in a normal 900-g/9 x 5-inch loaf pan instead, if you prefer.

BANANA BREAD IN A JAR

2 ripe bananas
110 g/1 stick butter
150 g/¾ cup caster/superfine sugar
2 eggs
225 g 1¾ cups self-raising/self-rising flour

40g/¼ cup chocolate chips (broken-up chocolate, leftover chocolate decorations) or chopped unsalted nuts of your choice

Makes 6 jars or 1 loaf

Preheat the oven to 140°C (275°F) Gas 1.

Mash the bananas. Cream the butter and sugar together until a pale cream colour and fluffy. Save your muscles and use a hand-held mixer for this. Add the eggs. Stir in the flour. Mix everything together. Fold in the chocolate chips or nuts.

Divide the mixture between 6 sterilized jars. They need to be filled just over a third full. Make sure there is no mixture spilled on the sides. Place on a baking sheet and bake in the preheated oven for about 35–40 minutes. They will be done when they have risen to just below the top and when an inserted skewer comes out clean. Cool slightly and screw the lid on.

If you are using a loaf pan, bake for about 50 minutes at 180°C (350°F) Gas 4.

Note
You will need 6 completely straight-sided jam/jelly jars as otherwise the cake won't slide out at the end (that is, unless you want to eat it straight from the jar). This is harder than it sounds, but straight-sided jars can be found online or Bonne Maman jars work well. Most glass jars are OK to cook on a low heat. Make sure the jar is thoroughly clean and sterilized before using to bake your cake.

INDEX

RECIPE CREDITS

Amanda Grant
Butternut squash soup
Cereal bars
Cheese straws
Chicken & red pepper stew
Chicken drumsticks
Egg Mayonnaise bagel
Falafel pockets
Fresh fruit jellies
Lemon shortbread
Mini quiches
Pesto cheese twists
Sausage & red pepper rolls
Smoked mackerel pâté
Spinach & onion tortilla
Turkey & cranberry wraps

Annie Rigg
Fizzy fruit jellies

Belinda Williams
Scottish root vegetable soup with pearl
   barley & thyme
Vegetable broth with chicken & kaffir lime

Carol Hilker
Steak ranchero burrito

Claire and Lucy McDonald
Banana bread in a jar
Gnocchi bake
Pulled pork rolls with apple butter
Speedy Gonzales noodles

Dunja Gulin
Fried tofu sandwiches

Helen Graves
Picnic loaf
Salmon & cream cheese bagel

Jenna Zoe
Baked tortilla chips with nectarine-tomato
   salsa
Creole cauliflower
Masala popcorn
No-bake crispie cakes
Oatmeal-raisin cookies
Orange, cardamom & hemp seed muffins
Peanut butter & jelly thumbprint cookies
Seeded amaranth crackers with beetroot/
   beet & herb dip
Spicy tomato kale chips

Jennie Shapter
Chicken Caesar wraps

Jenny Linford
Blush tomato & feta muffins
Tomato macaroni cheese

Jordan Bourke
Danish open-faced rye sandwiches
Leek, sprouting broccoli & chorizo tart
Quinoa with mint, orange & beets
Root vegetable fritters

Laura Washburn
African peanut & sweet potato soup
Avocado & chickpea wraps
Cheesy polenta & roasted vegetable pie
Clara's minestrone soup
Courgette/zucchini loaf
Creamy courgette/zucchini soup
Leek & Gruyère toastie
Puttanesca focaccia
Simple couscous salad
Simple pasta salad
Sweet potato, spinach & goat's cheese
   quesadilla
Tandoori chicken & paneer cheese
   naan-wich

Louise Pickford
'Pick me up' power bowl
Aloha seafood bento box
Alter-ego sushi
Fruit, honey & yogurt crunch jars
Healthy Moroccan bento box
Indian tiffin box
Instant chicken 'pot' noodle
Mexican olé bento box
Quick & easy jacket sweet potato
Really healthy Scotch egg
Spring pasta salad jar
Sunday leftover sandwiches
Sunday market salad jar

Nicola Graimes
Chickpea & spiced cauliflower salad with
   tamarind dressing
Marinated mushroom, crispy kale & rice
   salad
Seared lamb salad with pea, mint & radish

Tori Finch
Ham, pickled gherkin & lettuce wheels
Herby citrus quinoa jars
Proper salade niçoise
Salad of roasted root vegetables
The New York deli sandwich

Tori Haschka
Roast apple & pumpkin soup

PICTURE CREDITS

Peter Cassidy
Pages 7–9, 31, 70al, 90, 93l, 106, 107

Tara Fisher
Pages 11, 21, 33, 38, 52, 92br, 95, 99–103,
116br, 124, 126ar, 130, 133

Georgia Glynn-Smith
Pages 23, 47, 54, 58

Adrian Lawrence
Pages 1–5, 10bl, 13, 40a, 41r, 43, 44, 50, 65,
66–69, 73, 85, 89, 92a, 93r, 96, 111, 115, 129

Lisa Linder
Pages 126br, 131

Steve Painter
Pages 10al, 24, 27, 37, 51, 70ar, 71r, 77, 79

William Reavell
Pages 10ar, 19

Matt Russell
Pages 40bl, 41l, 57, 61, 62

Ian Wallace
Page 45

Stuart West
Pages 28, 40br, 53, 126al, 141

Kate Whitaker
Pages 6, 14, 22, 49, 70br, 71l, 81, 83, 86,
92bl, 104, 108, 112, 127r, 132

Rob White and Stephen Conroy
Pages 10br, 17, 34

Isobel Wield
Pages 70bl, 74

Clare Winfield
Pages 9, 42, 116a, 116bl, 117, 119–123,
126bl, 127l, 135, 137-139